Out of this world	44
The quaking Earth	46
Slips and faults	48
Tremendous tremors	50
Making waves	52
Seismic science	54
Building seismographs	56
Fieldwork	58
Measuring movements	60
To the rescue	62

HURRICANES, TORNADOES & WILD WEATHER — 64

What is weather?	66
Heat from the Sun	68
Measuring temperature	70
Climates of the world	72
Changing the temperature	74
El Niño and La Niña	76
Beating the heat	78
Where the weather is	80
In the air	82
Air on the move	84
Air pressure	86

Whirlwinds and tornadoes	88
Measuring the wind	90
Hurricanes and cyclones	92
The water cycle	94
Humidity	96
Looking at clouds	98
Rain and dew	100
Making rainbows	102
Thunder and lightning	104
Charging up	106
Flood and drought	108
Gauging the rain	110
Snow and ice	112
Coping with cold	114
Ice age or greenhouse?	116
Studying the weather	118
Your weather station	120

Glossary	122
Index	126
Acknowledgements	128

INTRODUCTION

FROM the moment the Earth was created nearly five billion years ago, all-powerful forces have been at work shaping it into the planet we know today. Once completely molten, the Earth slowly cooled, leaving a hard crust of solid rock.

But the Earth's crust is thin and fragile, and it overlies rock layers that are still hot and relatively soft. Slow-flowing currents within these hot, putty-like rock layers carry plates (sections) of the crust hither and thither. They make hot, molten rock spurt out of the crust, creating volcanoes. And they make the ground shudder and shake, creating earthquakes.

Volcanoes and earthquakes cause much havoc. The lava-flows from erupting volcanoes destroy everything in their path. The ash and fumes they give off can smother and kill, and, polluting the atmosphere, they can alter the climate. The most deadly earthquakes can cause immense devastation, obliterating whole towns and sometimes killing tens of thousands of people in a matter of seconds.

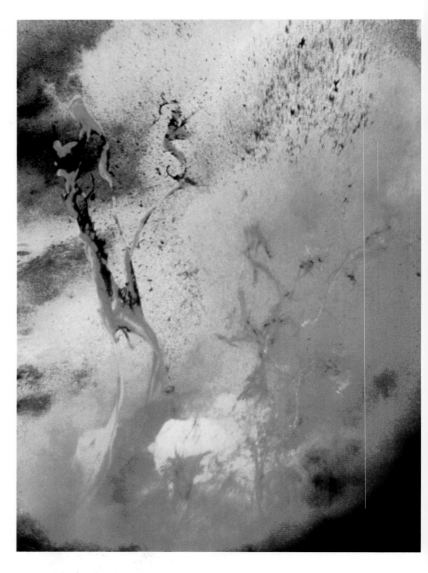

Above: Driven by powerful subterranean forces, molten lava erupts from a volcano and cascades down its slopes before disappearing into a boiling sea.

Left: When long periods of drought occur, lakes dry up, making life difficult, if not impossible, for wildlife and humans alike.

Right: Electricity builds up in towering storm clouds and flashes to Earth in a dazzling lightning display. The surrounding air expands explosively, creating the crackle and boom of thunder.

shaking earth

VOLCANOES, EARTHQUAKES, HURRICANES & TORNADOES

robin kerrod

southwater

This edition is published by Southwater

Southwater is an imprint of Anness Publishing Ltd,
Hermes House, 88-89 Blackfriars Road,
London SE1 8HA
tel. 020 7401 2077; fax 020 7633 9499
www.southwaterbooks.com; info@anness.com

UK agent: The Manning Partnership Ltd,
6 The Old Dairy, Melcombe Road,
Bath BA2 3LR; tel. 01225 478444;
fax 01225 478440; sales@manning-partnership.co.uk

UK distributor: Grantham Book Services Ltd,
Isaac Newton Way, Alma Park Industrial Estate,
Grantham, Lincs NG31 9SD; tel. 01476 541080;
fax 01476 541061; orders@gbs.tbs-ltd.co.uk

North American agent/distributor: National Book
Network, 4501 Forbes Boulevard, Suite 200, Lanham,
MD 20706; tel. 301 459 3366; fax 301 429 5746;
www.nbnbooks.com

Australian agent/distributor: Pan Macmillan Australia,
Level 18, St Martins Tower, 31 Market St, Sydney,
NSW 2000; tel. 1300 135 113; fax 1300 135 103;
customer.service@macmillan.com.au

New Zealand agent/distributor: David Bateman Ltd,
30 Tarndale Grove, Off Bush Road, Albany, Auckland;
tel. (09) 415 7664; fax (09) 415 8892

Publisher: Joanna Lorenz
Senior Editor: Lisa Miles
Editors: Leon Gray, Peter Harrison, Clare Gooden
and Elizabeth Woodland
Consultants: John Farndon and Helen Young
Designers: Caroline Reeves and Caroline Grimshaw
Jacket Design: Balley Design Associates
Photographer: John Freeman
Stylists: Thomasina Smith and Melanie Williams
Picture Researchers: Liz Eddison, Susannah Parker,
Gwen Campbell and Kay Rowley
Illustrators: Peter Bull Art Studio, Guy Smith
Production Controller: Darren Price

Previously published in
two separate volumes,
*Investigations: Wild
Weather* and
*Investigations: Volcanoes
& Earthquakes*

10 9 8 7 6 5 4 3 2 1

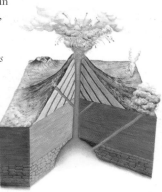

CONTENTS

Introduction   4

VOLCANOES & EARTHQUAKES   6

Fire from below   8

The active Earth   10

Eruption   12

Spreading seas   14

Moving magma   16

When plates meet   18

Hot spots   20

Cones and shields   22

Flowing lava   24

Vicious volcanoes   26

Dangerous gases   28

Mount St Helens   30

Volcanic rocks   32

Bubbles and intrusions   34

Volcanic landscapes   36

Letting off steam   38

Geysers and mudlarks   40

Changing climates   42

In Earth's early years, it was the gases and vapours spewed out by volcanoes that gave rise to our planet's first atmosphere. When water vapour in the atmosphere cooled and condensed, rain fell out of the sky to form the oceans. Today, the interchange of water between the atmosphere and the oceans, powered by heat from the Sun, largely governs the Earth's weather.

Like volcanoes and earthquakes, the weather can cause havoc in our world. The great storms that develop in tropical regions, like hurricanes and cyclones, unleash furious winds that can reach speeds of 200km/h. Across arid plains, the winds spiralling in tornadoes can reach more than twice this speed. Both hurricanes and tornadoes lay waste everything that lies in their path, snapping trees as if they were matchsticks and flattening buildings as if they were made of cards.

The lightning bolts and torrential rains that accompany the most devastating storms also take their toll of property and lives. But over the world as a whole, it is another facet of our weather – the lack of water, or drought – that accounts for the greatest loss of human life.

Largely because of global warming, world weather patterns seem to be becoming more unpredictable, with a greater incidence of destructive storms in some regions and more prolonged periods of drought in others. Whether we shall ever be able to alter or control the weather seems unlikely. For weather systems, like volcanoes and earthquakes, result from primeval, planet-wide forces that have been shaping the Earth since time began.

Above: Measuring hundreds of kilometres across, a hurricane powers its way across the Atlantic towards the coast of Florida and the island of Cuba.

Below: Although snow lies on the frozen ground in Yellowstone National Park, in Wyoming USA, the regular eruptions of Old Faithful geyser tell us that deep underground the rocks are scorching hot.

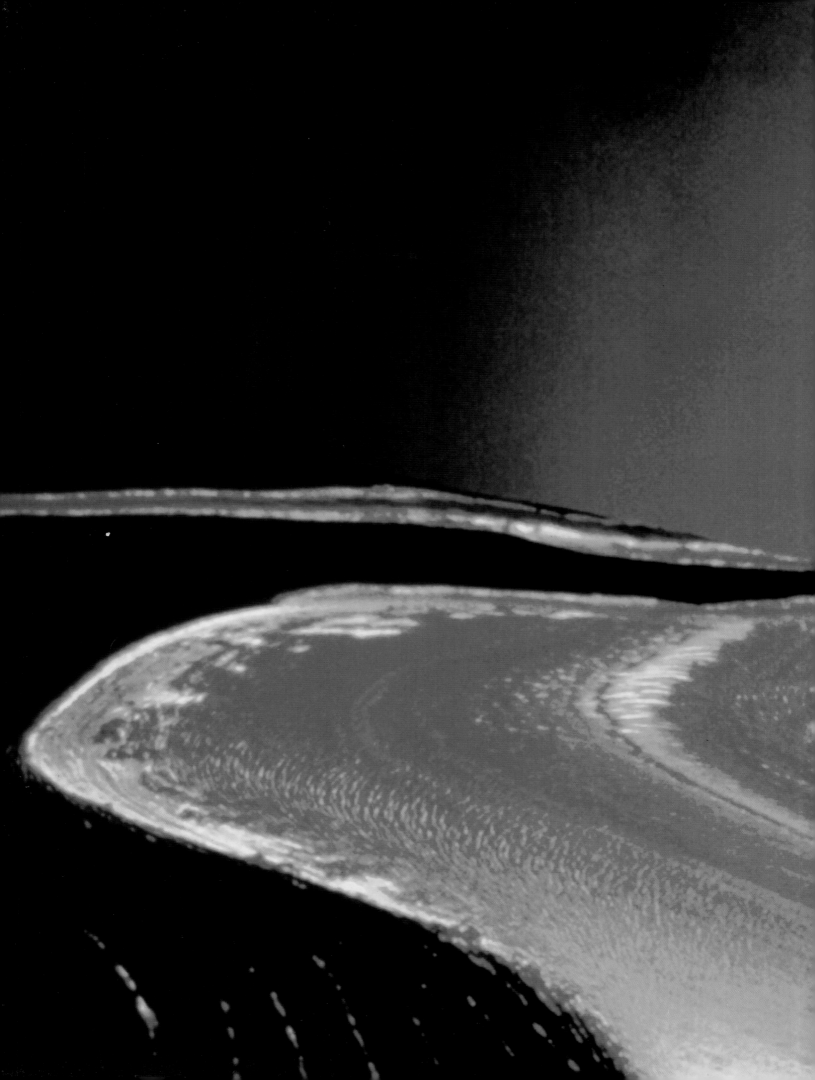

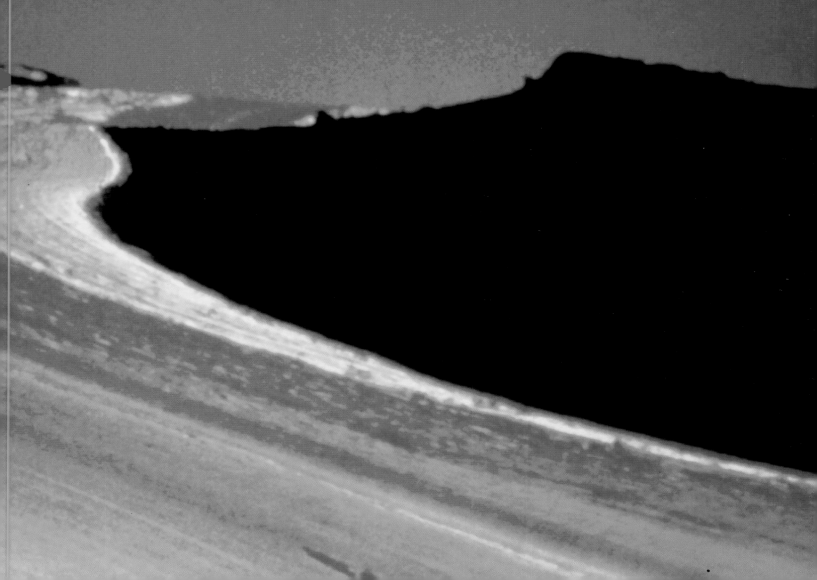

VOLCANOES & EARTHQUAKES

FIRE FROM BELOW

AT this moment in various parts of the world volcanoes are erupting. Fountains of red-hot rock are hurtling high into the air and rivers of lava are cascading down the volcanoes' sides. Volcanoes are places where molten (liquid) rock pushes up from below through splits in the Earth's crust. They may be beautiful but they can also be very destructive. Earthquakes are another destructive part of nature. Every year violent earthquakes destroy towns and kill hundreds, sometimes thousands, of people. The constant movements that take place in and beneath the rocky crust that covers the Earth cause volcanoes and earthquakes. The word volcano comes from the name that the people of ancient Rome gave to their god of fire. He was called Vulcan. Volcanology is the term given to the study of volcanoes and the scientists who study them are known as volcanologists.

The greatest
An artist's impression of the massive eruption of the volcano Krakatoa, near Java in south-east Asia, in 1883.

From the depths

When a volcano erupts, magma (red-hot molten rock) forces its way to the Earth's surface. It shoots into the air along with clouds of ash and gas, and runs out over the sides of the volcano. In time layers of ash and lava build up to form a huge cone shape.

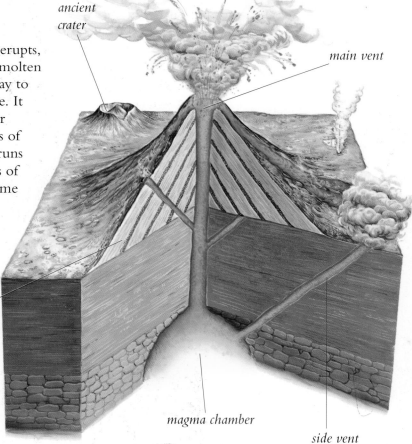

ancient crater

main vent

layers of lava and ash

magma chamber

side vent

FACT BOX

• The explosion of Krakatoa in Indonesia, in 1883 caused a massive tidal wave that killed 36,000 people.

• A powerful earthquake killed 5,500 people in the city of Kobe, Japan, in January 1995. Kobe was one of the largest ports in Japan and thousands of homes were destroyed. It was estimated it would take several years to rebuild the city completely.

Piping hot
Hot water often bubbles to the surface in volcanic regions. This creates geothermal (heated in the earth) springs. The hot spring pictured is in Yellowstone National Park in the USA.

Suited up
Heatproof suits and helmets like this make it possible for volcanologists to walk near red-hot lava. This volcanologist is taking samples of lava on the volcano Mauna Loa, on Hawaii.

Out of this world
There are huge volcanoes like this on the planet Venus. Volcanoes have helped shape many bodies in the Solar System, including Mars and the Moon.

Shaking earth
A badly-damaged village in India after a severe earthquake in 1993. Two plates (sections) of the Earth's crust meet in India. The plates push against each other and cause earthquakes.

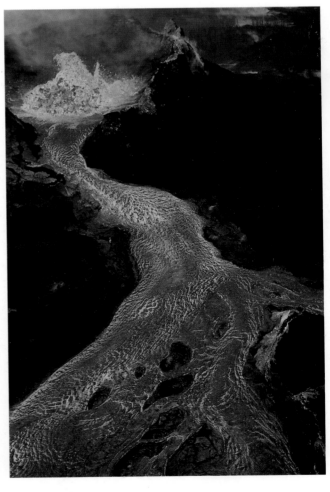

Red-hot river
A river of molten rock races down the sides of the Hawaiian volcano Kilauea in a 1994 eruption. Kilauea is one of the most active volcanoes known on Earth.

THE ACTIVE EARTH

THE causes of volcanoes and earthquakes begin many kilometres beneath the surface of the Earth. Our planet is covered with a thin layer of hard rock called the crust. Soil, in which trees and plants grow, has built up on top of the rock. Underneath the hard rock of the crust, however, there is a much hotter layer of the Earth called the mantle. The centre of the Earth, deep inside the mantle, is intensely hot. That heat moves out from the centre and heats everything in the mantle. In the mantle the rocks become semi-liquid and they move and flow like treacle. Because of the intense heat from the centre of the Earth, the rocks move in currents. Very hot liquid rocks (magma) are lighter than cooler rocks and float up towards the top of the mantle. Where there are gaps in the crust, the magma bubbles up through them and shoots out in volcanoes.

Volcanoes have been erupting on Earth for billions of years. During all that time they have pushed out enormous amounts of lava (magma pushed out of a volcano), ash and rocks. These hardened and built up in layers to form part of the landscapes around us. Volcanoes also produced water vapour that eventually condensed (turned to liquid) to form the Earth's seas and oceans.

The newborn Earth
Thousands of millions of years ago the Earth probably looked similar to the picture above. Molten rock was erupting from volcanoes everywhere on the Earth's surface, creating huge lava flows. These hardened into rocks.

Fit for giants
Looking like a spectacular, jumbled-up stairway, this rock formation is on the coast of County Antrim in Northern Ireland. It is known as the Giant's Causeway, because people in the past believed that giants built it. However, it is a natural formation made up of six-sided columns of basalt, one of the commonest volcanic rocks. Basalt often forms columns like these when it cools, and this is called columnar basalt. There are similar structures on Staffa, an island in the Inner Hebrides group off north-western Scotland. Among the many caves along Staffa's coastline is Fingal's Cave, about which the composer Mendelssohn wrote a famous overture.

Inside the Earth

The Earth is made up of a number of different layers. The top layer is the hard crust. It is thinnest under the oceans, where it is only some 5–10km thick. Underneath the crust there is a thick layer of semi-liquid rock known as the mantle. Beneath the mantle is a layer of liquid metal, mainly iron and nickel, that makes up the Earth's outer core. The inner core at the centre is solid, made up of iron and other metals.

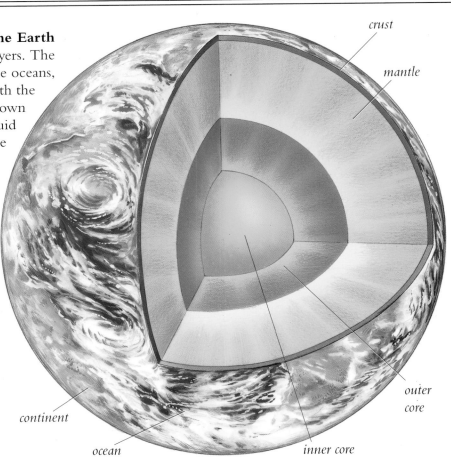

crust

mantle

outer core

inner core

ocean

continent

Fire and ice

This bleak landscape in Iceland was created by the country's many volcanoes. Iceland is one of the most volcanically active places in the world and hardened lava covers most of the country.

Iron from space

Iron is also found in meteorites that fall to our planet from space. This 60-tonne iron meteorite is the world's largest. It was found in 1920 at Hoba, Namibia, in south-west Africa. Scientists estimate that it fell to Earth about 80,000 years ago.

A rocky layer cake

There are other rocks on Earth besides those made by volcanoes. Sedimentary rocks were formed out of sediment, or material produced when older surface rocks were worn away by wind and rain. These kinds of rocks build up in layers. This picture of the Grand Canyon in the USA shows an enormous area of sedimentary rocks. You can see how they are built up in layers of different colours.

ERUPTION

PEOPLE usually think of volcanoes as mountains of fire that shoot fountains of red-hot rock high into the air and pour out rivers of lava. But much more comes out of volcanoes besides molten rock. Water that has been heated and turned into a gas in the volcano comes out as water vapour and steam. Once it is outside the volcano the vapour cools down and condenses (turns back into water). The hot rock inside volcanoes produces many other kinds of gas, such as carbon dioxide. Some of these gases go into the air outside the volcano and some are mixed with the lava that flows from it. The second project shows you how to make a volcano that gives out lava mixed with carbon dioxide. As you will see, the red floury lava from your volcano comes out frothing, full of bubbles of this gas. In a real volcano, it is the gas that is mixed with the lava that makes the volcano suddenly explode. The gas bubbles and swells inside the volcano and pushes out the mixture of lava and gas violently.

Hawaiian fire
The gigantic Hawaiian volcano Mauna Loa erupted in 1984, sending rivers of red-hot lava cascading down its slopes. The lava came dangerously close to the coastal town of Hilo. If the lava had reached Hilo, the town would have been set on fire.

WATER VAPOUR

You will need: heat-proof jug, saucepan, oven glove, plate.

1 Fill up the jug with water from the hot tap. Pour the water into the saucepan. Switch on one of the hotplates or light a gas ring on a cooker and place the saucepan on it.

2 Heat the water in the saucepan until it is boiling hard and steam is coming from it. Pick up the plate with the oven gloves and hold it upside-down above the saucepan.

3 After a few minutes, turn off the cooker and take the plate away using the oven gloves. You will see that the plate is covered with drops of water. This water is water vapour (steam) that has cooled and turned back to liquid.

1 Make sure the jug is dry, or the mixture will stick to the sides. Empty the baking soda into the jug and add the flour. Thoroughly mix the two using the stirrer.

ERUPTION

You will need: *jug, baking soda, flour, stirring rod, funnel, plastic bottle, sand, seed tray (without holes), large plastic bin lid, vinegar, red food colouring.*

2 Place the funnel in the neck of the plastic bottle. Again, make sure that the funnel is perfectly dry first. Now pour in the mixture of soda and flour from the jug.

3 Empty sand into the tray until it is half-full. Fill the jug with water and pour it into the tray to make the sand sticky but not too wet. Mix together with the stirring rod.

4 Stand the bottle containing the flour and soda mixture in the centre of the plastic lid. Then start packing the wet sand around it. Make the sand into a cone shape.

7 The sandy volcano you have made will begin to erupt. The vinegar and soda mix to give off carbon dioxide. This makes the flour turn frothy and forces it out of the bottle as red lava.

5 Pour the vinegar into the jug. Then add enough food colouring to make the vinegar a rich red colour. White wine vinegar will make a richer colour.

6 Place the funnel in the mouth of the plastic bottle and quickly pour into it the red-coloured vinegar in the jug. Now remove the funnel from the bottle.

SPREADING SEAS

THE Earth's crust is not all in one piece. but is made up of many sections, called plates. They are solid and float on currents circulating in the deep layer of semi-liquid rock beneath them in the mantle. All the plates of the crust move in different directions. Some plates are moving apart and others are moving towards one another. The plates that move apart are usually under the oceans. Magma pushes up from below the sea-floor and squeezes through gaps between the edges of the ocean plates. The magma squeezing up pushes the plates in opposite directions. As the plates move apart they make the ocean floor wider and push continents apart. This is known as sea-floor spreading. Sea-floor spreading builds up plates because when the magma cools it adds new rock at the edges of the plates. This kind of boundary between two plates is called a constructive boundary. The magma pushes up the seabed to form a long mountain range called a ridge or rise. Ridges are very noticeable features on the floors of both the Atlantic and the Pacific Oceans.

Underwater explorer
The deep-diving research submersible (midget submarine) *Alvin*. The submersible can carry a pilot and two scientific observers to a depth of 4,000m. *Alvin* can dive so deeply that scientists were able to study the Mid-Atlantic Ridge. The submersible also helped scientists to discover mineral deposits on the ocean floor.

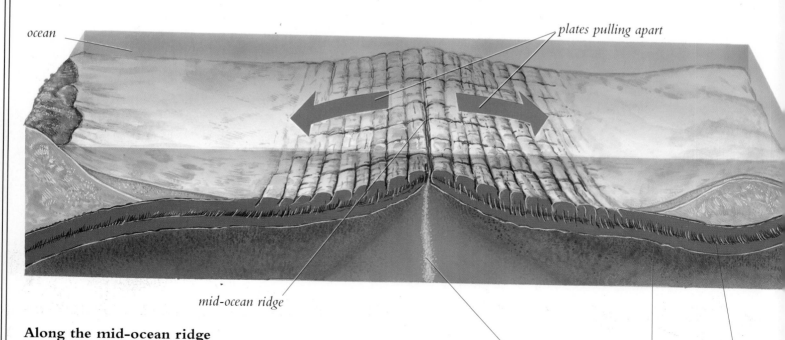

ocean   *plates pulling apart*

mid-ocean ridge

rising magma   *mantle*   *plate*

Along the mid-ocean ridge
A mid-ocean ridge forms when molten magma pushes its way upwards from the mantle, the semi-molten layer under the crust. The magma bubbles up through cracks in the crust as they are pulled apart. When the magma meets the sea water it hardens to form ridges.

Strange life

Hot water full of minerals streams out of the vents (openings) along the mid-ocean ridges. Strange creatures live around them. They include the giant tube worms pictured here around vents in the Galapagos Islands in the eastern Pacific Ocean. Other creatures that thrive on the ridges include species of blind crabs and shrimps.

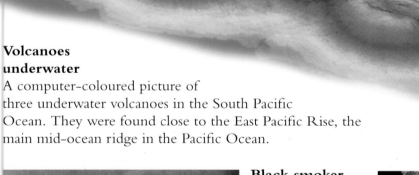

Volcanoes underwater

A computer-coloured picture of three underwater volcanoes in the South Pacific Ocean. They were found close to the East Pacific Rise, the main mid-ocean ridge in the Pacific Ocean.

New island

The island of Surtsey, off Iceland, did not exist before November 1963. In that month the top of an erupting volcano broke through the sea's surface close to Iceland. The volcano continued erupting for more than three years. There were times when the ash and steam rising from the new volcano reached more than 5km into the sky.

Black smoker

Water as hot as 350°C, hotter than a domestic oven, pours out of vents along the ocean ridges. The water often contains particles of black sulphur minerals that make it look like smoke. This is why these vents are called black smokers.

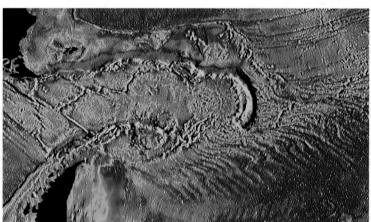

Plate and sandwich

A satellite view showing a small ocean plate on the floor of the South Atlantic Ocean between the tip of South America (top left) and Antarctica (bottom left). The curved shape in the centre is the South Sandwich Trench.

MOVING MAGMA

PLASTIC FLOW

You will need: *lump of modelling clay, wooden board.*

THE temperature of the rocks in the Earth's mantle can be as high as 1,500°C. At this temperature the rocks would normally melt. They are under such pressure from the rocks above them that they cannot melt completely. They are, however, able to flow slowly. This is like a solid piece of modelling clay that flows slightly when you put enough pressure on it. This kind of flow is called plastic flow. In places, the rocks in the upper part of the mantle do melt completely. This melted rock, called magma, collects in huge pockets called magma chambers. The magma rises because it is hotter and lighter than the semi-liquid rocks. Volcanoes form above magma chambers when the hot magma can rise to the surface. The second project demonstrates this principle using hot and cold water. The hot water rises through the cold because it is lighter.

1 Make sure that the table is protected by a sheet. Knead the lump of clay in your hands until it is quite flexible. Now shape it into a ball. Place it on the table.

Rock currents
Underneath the Earth's hard crust, the rock is semi-liquid and can move slowly. It moves in currents. Hot rock moves upwards and cooler rock sinks back down.

2 Place the wooden board on top of the ball of clay and press down. The clay flattens and squeezes out at the sides. It is just like semi-liquid rock flowing under pressure.

3 Roll the clay into a ball again and press it with the board. But this time push the board forwards at the same time. The clay will again flow and allow the board to move forwards. The board is moving in the same way as the plates in the Earth's crust move.

1 Pour some of the food colouring into the small jar. You may need to add more later to give your solution a deep colour. This will make the last stage easier to see.

2 Fill the small jug with water from the hot tap. Pour it into the small jar. Fill it right to the brim, but not to overflowing. Wipe off any that spills down the sides.

3 Cut a circular patch from the plastic food wrapping a few centimetres bigger than the top of the small jar. Place it over the top and secure it with the elastic band.

BLACK SMOKERS

You will need: *dark food colouring, small jar (such as baby food jar), small jug, transparent plastic food wrapping, strong elastic band, sharpened pencil, large jar, oven gloves, large jug.*

4 With the sharp end of the pencil, carefully make two small holes in the plastic covering the top of the jar. If any coloured water splashes out, wipe it off.

6 Watch what happens. The coloured hot water begins rising from the holes. This happens because the hot water is lighter, or less dense, than the cold water around it.

5 Now place the small jar inside the larger one. Use oven gloves because it is hot. Fill the large jug with cold water and pour it into the large jar, not into the small one.

WHEN PLATES MEET

THE plates on the sea floor that spread out from the mid-ocean ridges meet edge-to-edge with the plates carrying the continents. The edges of the plates then push against each other. Because continental rock is lighter than ocean-floor rock, the edge of the continental plate rides up over the edge of the ocean plate. The ocean plate is then forced back into the mantle inside the Earth. As the ocean plate goes down into the mantle, it melts and is gradually destroyed. This kind of boundary between colliding plates is called a destructive boundary because the edge of the ocean plate is destroyed. Where the ocean plate starts to descend, a deep trench forms in the sea-bed. The continental plate is also affected by the ocean plate pushing against it. It wrinkles up and ranges of fold mountains are formed. The great mountain chains of North and South America – the Rockies and the Andes – were formed in this way. Earthquakes also occur at destructive boundaries. So do volcanoes, as parts of the destroyed ocean plate force their way through the weakened continental crust.

Around the Pacific

Most of the Pacific Ocean sits on one huge plate moving north-west. This rubs against other plates and creates a huge arc of volcanoes (shown in red) along the plate edges.

continental crust wrinkles up

ocean trench

ocean

ocean plate

continental plate

ocean plate descends

FACT BOX

• The Andes Mountains of South America were formed by the collision between the South American plate and the Nazca plate. With a length of nearly 9,000km, they form the longest mountain range in the world.

• The deepest part of the world's oceans is Challenger Deep, which lies in the Marianas Trench in the North Pacific Ocean. The depth there is almost 11km.

Along ocean trenches

In many places around the world, a plate moving away from an ocean ridge meets a plate carrying a continent. When this happens, the ocean plate (which is made up of heavier material) is forced down underneath the continental plate. This causes a deep trench to form where the plates meet.

Youngest and tallest

The Himalayas in southern Asia form the highest mountain range in the world. They include Mount Everest which, at 8,848m, is the Earth's highest single peak. The range began rising only about 50 million years ago. The plate carrying India collided with the Asia plate at that time. The Himalayas is one of the youngest mountain ranges on Earth. In the long history of the Earth, 50 million years is not a particularly long time.

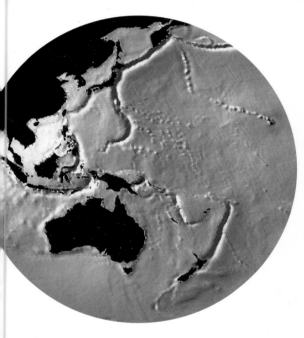

The ocean trenches

This satellite photograph of the Earth shows Australia at lower centre with the huge land mass of Asia at the top of the globe. The North and South Pacific Oceans are to the right, while the Indian Ocean is on the left. Variations in the height of the sea surface are clearly visible. The surface dips in places where there are deep trenches on the ocean bed many kilometres below. The deep trenches to the right of Australia in this view are the Kermadek and Tonga Trenches. The Marianas Trench is upper centre.

Volcanoes on the edge

The volcano on White Island, off the North Island of New Zealand lies close to an ocean trench, where the Pacific plate is descending. As the plate descends, it heats up and changes back to magma. This forces its way to the surface as a volcano. White Island volcano is one of hundreds that ring the Pacific Ocean. Together they form a ring of volcanoes which is called the Ring of Fire.

Above the clouds

The tops of volcanoes rise above the clouds on the Indonesian island of Java. Most of the country's islands lie near the edge of a descending plate and have active volcanoes.

HOT SPOTS

Powerful Pele
This is the name of the fire goddess of Hawaii. According to legend, Pele lives in a crater at the summit of the volcano Kilauea. When she wishes she melts the rocks and pours out flows of lava that destroy everything in their path. When Pele stamps her feet, the Earth trembles.

FACT BOX

• The Hawaiian hot-spot volcano of Mauna Kea is 9,000m high from the ocean floor. That is nearly 1,000m taller than Mount Everest. Half of Mauna Kea is below sea level.

• When sea mount volcanoes die, they cool and shrink. It is possible that the legendary lost city of Atlantis could have been built on top of a flat sea mount. Then the sea mount shrank and Atlantis sank beneath the waves.

MOST of the world's volcanoes lie at the edges of plates. A few volcanoes, however, such as those in Hawaii, are a long way from the plate edges. They lie over hot spots beneath the Earth's crust. A hot spot is an area on a plate where hot rock from the mantle bubbles up underneath. While the plate above moves, the hot spot stays in the same place in the mantle. The hot spot keeps burning through the plate to make a volcano in a new place. A string of dead volcanoes is left behind as the plate moves over the hot spot. Some form islands above the ocean surface. Others, called sea mounts, remain submerged. The best known active volcanoes far from plate boundaries are Kilauea and Mauna Loa on the main island of Hawaii. The Hawaiian archipelago lies in the middle of the Pacific plate, thousands of kilometres from plate boundaries. Its volcanoes erupt because it lies directly above a hot spot. The other Hawaiian islands formed over the same hot spot but were carried away by plate movement. In time, the main island will be carried away also. Volcanoes erupting from the hot spot will create a new island to take its place. The island of Réunion in the Indian Ocean is another example of a hot-spot location.

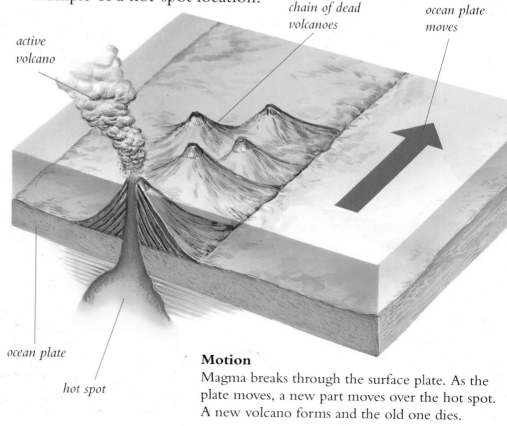

active volcano

chain of dead volcanoes

ocean plate moves

ocean plate

hot spot

Motion
Magma breaks through the surface plate. As the plate moves, a new part moves over the hot spot. A new volcano forms and the old one dies.

Islands in line

Astronauts took this picture of the Hawaiian island chain in the North Pacific from the space shuttle *Discovery* in 1998. This island group is formed over a hot spot on the Pacific plate. The largest island is Hawaii which appears at the top of this picture.

Lanzarote's lunar landscape

Huge volcanic eruptions took place on Lanzarote, another Canary Island, in the 1800s and 1900s. They covered most of the island with lava and ash. The landscape is similar to the landscape on the Moon. Very few plants can grow in a landscape of this kind. Lanzarote has more than 300 volcanic craters. Many are to be seen in the area of the most recent lava flows, in the spectacular "Mountains of Fire".

Canary hot spot

Snow-capped Mount Teide, the highest peak on Tenerife, in the Canary Islands. It rises to 3,718m and was formed 10 million years ago by volcanic activity over the Canary Islands' hot spot. Teide last erupted in 1909.

Pacific atoll

There are many ring-shaped coral islands, or atolls, in the Pacific Ocean. These began as coral grew around the mouth of a volcano that rose above the ocean's surface. The the volcano sank, but the coral went on growing.

Pele is angry!

The volcano Kilauea, on Hawaii, is shown erupting here. At such times Hawaiians say that their fire goddess Pele is angry. She is supposed to live in Kilauea's crater. Kilauea, on the main island of Hawaii, is located over a hot spot on the Pacific plate. It formed only about 700,000 years ago.

CONES AND SHIELDS

Sticky rock

A volcano erupts with explosive force on Bali. It is one of a string of islands that make up Indonesia. There are more than 130 active volcanoes on the islands. They all pour out the sticky type of lava Hawaiians call aa.

AROUND the world there are more than 1,000 active volcanoes. They are all very different. Some erupt fairly quietly and send out rivers of molten lava that can travel for many kilometres. Others erupt with explosive violence, blowing out huge clouds of ash. The kind of magma inside a volcano makes the difference between it being quiet or explosive. Quiet volcanoes, such as those that form on the ocean ridges and over hot spots have magma with very little gas in it. The Hawaiian volcanoes formed over a hot spot. Their lava flows far, and they grow very broad. They are called shield volcanoes. Explosive volcanoes have magma inside them that is full of gas. Gas pressure can build up inside a volcano until it explodes. This is the kind of volcano found in the Ring of Fire around the Pacific plate. Because of their shape these volcanoes are called cone volcanoes. The blast and ash clouds these volcanoes give off can and do kill hundreds of people. The ash clouds can even cause changes in the weather. Large clouds of dust in the Earth's atmosphere from volcanoes block out the Sun's heat, making the weather on Earth colder.

Red river

A river of molten lava flows down the slopes of the volcano Kilauea on the main island of Hawaii. Like the other volcanoes on the island, Kilauea is a shield volcano. It pours out very runny lava that flows for long distances, usually at speeds up to about 100m an hour. The fastest lava flows are called by their Hawaiian name of pahoehoe.

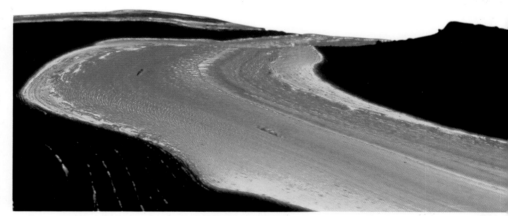

Long mountain

The volcano Mauna Loa on the main island of Hawaii is of 4,170m high. It is a shield-type volcano, meaning it is broad, with gently sloping sides. The main dome measures 120km across and its lava flows stretch for more than 5,000 sq km. In the Hawaiian language, the name means Long Mountain. This is a good name for it because it is very long and is the biggest mountain mass in the world.

Building layers

Explosive volcanoes blast rock and ash into the air. These eventually fall to the ground and lie there. Geologists call the rock and ash on the ground tephra. Here on Mount Teide, in Tenerife, layers of tephra have built up on top of each other after repeated eruptions.

Sacred mountain

Snow-covered Mount Fuji on the island of Honshu, Japan. Also called Fujiyama, it is one of the most beautiful volcanoes in the world and is considered sacred by the Japanese. It has an almost perfect cone shape. Five lakes ring the base of the volcano.

At the top

The caldera (crater) at the summit of the volcano Kilauea, on the island of Hawaii. There are vents (holes) in the caldera from which lava flows. The most active vent in the caldera is named Halemaumau. This is the legendary home of the fire goddess Pele.

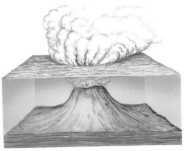

Submarine (undersea) volcanoes may grow in size until they rise above the surface of the sea. Scientists believe that this is how atolls are formed.

Hawaiian volcanoes have runny lava and gentle slopes

Strombolian volcanoes spit out lava bombs in small explosions.

Plinian volcanoes produce thick, gassy lava and shoot columns of ash high into the air.

Fissure volcanoes are giant cracks in the ground from which lava flows.

Vulcanian volcanoes produce thick, sticky lava and erupt with violent explosions.

Pelean volcanoes produce clouds of very hot ash and gases. These clouds are dense and roar or gush quickly downhill.

Volcano types

Although all volcanoes behave in different ways, we can group them into a number of different kinds. In fissure volcanoes, magma forces its way up through long cracks in the Earth's crust. Then it flows out on either side and cools to form broad plateaus. Other volcanoes grow in various shapes caused by how runny or thick their lava is. Some of these volcanoes are famous for their violent eruptions of thick clouds of ash and gas.

FLOWING LAVA

LAVA VISCOSITY

You will need: two paper plates, jar of liquid honey, pen, stopwatch, jug of ordinary washing-up liquid.

1 Mark a large circle on the plates by drawing around the edge of a saucer. Pour a tablespoon of honey from the jar into the middle of the circle. Start the stopwatch.

IN some parts of the world, there are ancient lava flows that are hundreds of kilometres long. Long flows like these have come from fissures (cracks) in the crust, which have poured out runny lava. Runny lava is much thinner than the lava produced by explosive volcanoes, which is sometimes called pasty lava. The correct name for the thickness of a liquid is viscosity. Thin liquids have a low viscosity, thick liquids a high viscosity. The first project below investigates the different viscosities of two liquids and how differently they flow. The second project looks at at the effect on substances of temperature. Heating solids to a sufficiently high temperature makes them first turn soft, then melt and then flow. Rock is no exception to this rule. If you make rock hot enough it softens, becomes liquid, and then flows. Deep inside a volcano, hot rock becomes liquid and flows up and out onto the surface as lava. When the lava comes out, its temperature can be as high as 1,200°C This is the temperature of most of the runny lavas of the Hawaiian shield volcanoes. There are two kinds of lava flows from these volcanoes. One is called pahoehoe and the other aa by the Hawaiians. Volcanologists use these names for similar flows the world over. Pahoehoe and aa flows have different kinds of surfaces. Pahoehoe has quite a smooth skin and wrinkles up like coils of rope. Aa flows have a very much rougher surface that is full of rubble.

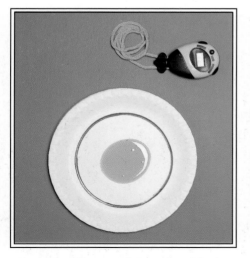

2 After 30 seconds, mark with the pen how far the honey has run. After another 30 seconds mark again. Stop the watch when the honey has reached the circle.

3 Part-fill the jug with washing-up liquid and pour some into the centre of another plate. Use the same amount as the honey you poured. Start the stopwatch.

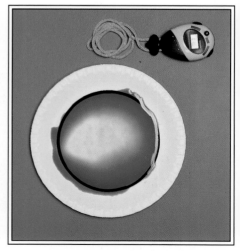

4 After 30 seconds, note how far the liquid has run. You will probably find that it has reached the circle. It flows faster because it has a much lower viscosity than honey.

MAGMA TEMPERATURE

You will need: *block of hard cooking margarine, jam jar, jug, large mixing bowl, stopwatch.*

1 Scoop out some margarine and drop it onto the bottom of the jar. For the best results, use hard cooking margarine, not a soft margarine spread.

2 Pick up the jar and tilt it slightly. See what happens to the margarine. The answer is, not a lot. It sticks to the bottom of the jar and does not slide down.

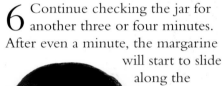

6 Continue checking the jar for another three or four minutes. After even a minute, the margarine will start to slide along the bottom as it warms and starts to melt. After several minutes, it is quite fluid.

3 Fill the jug with hot water and pour some into the bowl. Shake it around to heat the bowl, then pour it away. Now pour the rest of the hot water into the bowl.

4 Pick up the jar and tilt it again. The margarine still will not move. Now place the jar on the bottom of the bowl. Keep your fingers clear of the hot water.

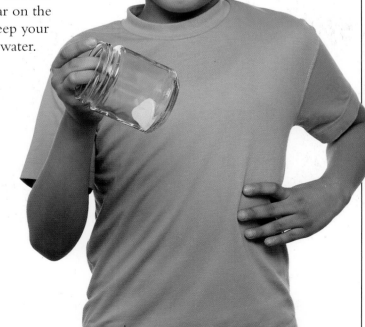

5 Start the stopwatch and after one minute, take out the jar. Tilt it, and see if the margarine moves. Return it to the bowl and after another minute, look at it again.

VICIOUS VOLCANOES

ERUPTING volcanoes can be among the most impressive sights in nature. They are almost always destructive, however, and can be deadly. Quiet volcanoes are the least dangerous to life, but their lava flows will destroy anything in their path. Explosive volcanoes are the most destructive. Their lava does not flow far because it is so thick. However, the clouds of ash, shattered rock and gas they blast out can be deadly. It was an exceptionally heavy ash fall that killed people by the thousand in ancient Pompeii. When the volcanoes explode first, they often give off a glowing cloud of white-hot ash, gas, and rocky debris. This is called a *nuée ardente* (glowing avalanche) and can travel at speeds of up to 100 km/h. Such a cloud killed tens of thousands in St Pierre in the Caribbean in 1902. The gases that all volcanoes give out can also be deadly. They include sulphur dioxide and hydrogen sulphide. Both gases are highly poisonous. Vast amounts of carbon dioxide are also given off. This is not poisonous in itself, but it can kill by suffocation (inability to breathe). The carbon dioxide blocks out oxygen. When there is no oxygen, people cannot breathe. In 1986, more than 1,500 people and many animals died in this way at Lake Nyos in Cameroon.

Menace on Montserrat
Ash clouds billow high into the sky from this volcano in the Soufrière Hills on the Caribbean island of Montserrat early in 1997. Many people had to flee from the island.

plaster casts of bodies

Long ago in Herculaneum
The excavated remains of one of the houses in the Roman town of Herculaneum, near Naples in Italy. It was destroyed at the same time as nearby Pompeii in August AD79. It was blasted by hot gas and buried by repeated avalanches of hot ash and rock from Vesuvius.

The Garden of Fugitives
In this part of the excavated city of Pompeii plaster casts of victims of the AD79 eruption of Vesuvius are displayed. Their life-like casts show how they huddled together in fear.

The death of Pompeii

On 24 August AD79, Mount Vesuvius, near Naples in Italy, erupted with explosive violence. A huge, choking cloud of gas, hot ash, and cinders blew down and covered the Roman town of Pompeii. At least 2,000 people are thought to have been killed either in their homes, or trying to flee from the deadly cloud. In a short time most of the city was buried. Over the past century more than half of the city has been uncovered. The ash and cinders have been dug away from many different buried buildings.

Silent killer

Carbon dioxide killed these cattle in fields near Lake Nyos, in Cameroon. The gas was released during a volcanic explosion under the lake in August 1986.

Lava rain

Volcanic bombs on the slopes of Mount Teide, on Tenerife, in the Canary Islands. They were thrown out during an eruption of the volcano as lumps of partly molten lava.

Gas sampling

A volcanologist takes a sample of gases from a volcanic vent. He wears a gas mask to avoid being suffocated.

Indian burial

The cinder field around Sunset Crater in Arizona, USA. The volcano that created the crater erupted in about AD1064. Thick lava flows, fumaroles (gas vents) and ice caves have been found in the surrounding area. It has been a US national park since 1930.

FACT BOX

- In April 1815 on the island of Sumbawa, in Indonesia, the volcano Tambora exploded. An estimated 90,000 people died directly from the eruption or from famine caused by ruined crops.

- In May 1902, a glowing cloud of gas from the Mount Pelée volcano on the Caribbean island of Martinique destroyed the city of St Pierre and killed its 30,000 inhabitants.

DANGEROUS GASES

THE two projects here look at two effects the gases given out by volcanoes can have. In the first project you will see how the build up of gas pressure can blow up a balloon. If you have put enough gas-making mixture in the bottle, the balloon may explode. Be careful. When the gas pressure builds up inside a volcano, an enormous explosion takes place, often releasing a deadly hot gas cloud like the one that killed thousands of people in Pompeii. The second project shows the effect of carbon dioxide, a gas often given out by volcanoes. The project uses the gas to prevent oxygen reaching a candle. The candle cannot burn without oxygen. This explains how carbon dioxide kills people by suffocation: it stops oxygen getting into their lungs. The project also shows that carbon dioxide is heavier than air. Being heavy makes it dangerous because clouds of the gas can push away the air from around people and animals.

GAS PRESSURE

You will need: funnel, drinks bottle, baking soda, vinegar, jug, balloon.

Plaster casts

Gas killed many of those who died at Pompeii. Archaeologists (people who study the past) can recreate the shapes of their bodies. First they fill hollows left by the bodies with wet plaster of Paris and let it harden. Then they remove the cast from the rock in which the bodies fell.

1 Make sure the funnel is dry first. Place it in the top of the bottle and pour in some baking soda. Now pour the vinegar into the funnel from the jug and into the bottle.

2 Remove the funnel. Quickly fit the neck of the balloon over the top of the bottle. Notice that the vinegar and soda are fizzing and giving off bubbles of gas.

3 The balloon starts to blow up because of the pressure, or force, of the gas in the bottle. The more gas given out, the more the balloon fills. Don't burst the balloon!

SUFFOCATING GAS

You will need: *funnel, bottle, baking soda, vinegar, jug, modelling clay, pencil, long straw, tall and short candles, large jar, matches.*

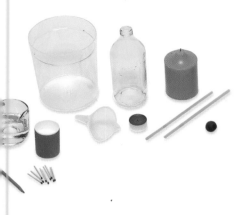

1 Place the funnel in the bottle and add the baking soda. Pour in the vinegar from the jug. This bottle is your gas generator. The gas produced is carbon dioxide.

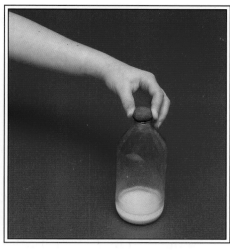

2 Knead a piece of modelling clay until it is soft, then push it into the mouth of the bottle. Make sure it fits tightly. This will make sure that no gas will escape past it.

3 Make a hole in the clay stopper with the pencil. Carefully push the straw through the hole. Press the clay around the straw.

Deadly fumes
Clouds of poisonous sulphur fumes billow out from holes on the slopes of Mount Etna, on the Italian island of Sicily. It is one of the most active volcanoes in the world.

4 Stand both candles in the bottom of the large jar. Ask an adult to light them. Light the short one first to avoid the danger of being burned if the tall candle were lit first.

5 Direct the straw of your gas generator into the bottom of the jar. Keep your arms well away from the candle flames. Soon you will find that the short candle goes out. The carbon dioxide gas has covered it and blocked out the oxygen that would let it burn.

MOUNT ST HELENS

Picture perfect
Mount St Helens before the May 1980 eruption.

Mount St Helens lies in the Cascade range of mountains near the north-west coast of the USA. This mountain range includes many volcanoes. Before 1980, Mount St Helens had not erupted for 130 years. The mountain began to shake in March 1980. Scientists knew there was about to be an eruption. Many scientists and tourists travelled to photograph what would happen. The progress of the eruption was recorded by hosts of people on the ground, in the air and also by satellite. Nothing prepared the geologists who had gathered there, for the spectacular explosion on the morning of 18 May 1980, however. The blast, the ash clouds, the rain of debris from the volcano, the mud slides, and the poisonous fumes killed 60 people that morning. When the clouds cleared, the mountain had lost 430m in height and acquired a crater 3km across. Mount St Helens was no longer a beautiful piece of tourist scenery.

Blast off
An enormous cloud of thick ash billows from the huge new crater formed when the top of Mount St Helens blew off on 18 May 1980. The cloud rose to a height of more than 20km. It dropped ash over the surrounding region and on towns far away as it blew towards them. In some towns the ash blocked out the Sun. The city of Yakima was particularly badly hit. Over 500,000 tonnes of ash later had to be removed from the area surrounding Mount St Helens.

Before and after
These satellite photographs of the Mount St Helens region were taken before and after the eruption. They show how much land was devastated and covered by ash. The picture on the left was taken a few months before the eruption occurred. The mountain's snow cap is beginning to grow as autumn sets in. The picture on the right was taken about a year after the eruption. Ash covers thousands of hectares of what was once forest land.

Like ninepins

This photograph shows what remained of a forest on the slopes of Mount St Helens after it erupted. Thousands of trees were knocked over by the powerful blast. In places the fallen trees were swept away by an avalanche of rocks, dust and mud, which caused even greater destruction.

Ominous dome

Since the 1980 eruption, Mount St Helens has been quiet. Domes like this near the summit show that magma is still pushing up to the top of the volcano, however. This shows that it is still active.

Blooming again

Only a year after the eruption in 1980, plants are making a comeback on Mount St Helens. Flowers are blooming again on slopes washed clean by rain, and shrubs are pushing their way through the ash.

FACT BOX

• Native Americans of the Pacific Northwest called Mount St Helens *Tah-one-lat-clah* (fire mountain).

• Mount St Helens was previously active between 1832 and 1857.

• The first indication of a forthcoming eruption occurred on 20 March 1980, when an earthquake measuring over 4 on the Richter scale was recorded in the Mount St Helens area.

• On 27 March an explosion rocked the area, caused by an eruption of steam.

• Mount St Helens blew up at precisely 8.32 on the morning of 18 May 1980.

• The crater formed by the eruption measured 3.8km long and 1.9km wide.

Dark as night

Seven hours after Mount St Helens blew, street lighting was needed 140km away in the town of Yakima because the air was filled with black, choking dust.

VOLCANIC ROCKS

THE lava that flows out of volcanoes eventually cools, hardens and becomes solid rock. Volcanoes can give off several different kinds of lava that form different kinds of rocks. All these rocks are known as igneous, or fire-formed rocks, because they were born in the fiery heart of volcanoes. They contrast with sedimentary rock, the other main kind of rock found in the Earth's crust. This was formed from layers of silt that built up in ancient rivers and seas. Two of the main kinds of igneous rocks formed by volcanoes are basalt and andesite. Basalt is the rock most often formed from runny lava. This kind of lava pours out of the volcanoes on the ocean ridges and over hot spots. It is dark and dense. Andesite is the rock most often formed from the pasty lava that comes out of the explosive volcanoes on destructive plate boundaries. Because the crystals in both rocks are very small, they are called fine-grained rocks.

Road block
Lava flowing from the Kilauea volcano on Hawaii has cut off one of the island's roads. When the flow stopped, the molten lava had solidified into black volcanic rock with a smooth surface.

Intrusions
Here in Lanzarote, in the Canary Islands, molten rock has intruded, or forced its way through, other rock layers and then hardened. When this happens, geologists call it an intrusion. Volcanic intrusions like this most often occur underground when molten rock forces its way towards the surface. Sheet-like intrusions are known as dykes if they are vertical. If intrusions are horizontal and form between the rock layers, or strata, geologists call them sills.

Obsidian

This volcanic rock is formed when lava cools very quickly. It looks like black glass and is often called volcanic glass.

Basalt

Dark, heavy basalt is one of the most common volcanic rocks. This sample is known as vesicular basalt because it is riddled with holes.

Andesite

Andesite is a lighter-coloured rock than basalt. It is so-called because it is the typical rock found in the Andes Mountains.

Rhyolite

This is another fine-grained rock like basalt and andesite. It is much lighter in colour and weight than the other two, however.

Pumice

Pumice is a very light rock that is full of holes. It forms when lava containing a lot of gas pours out of underwater volcanoes.

Tuff

Tuff is rock formed from the ash ejected in volcanic eruptions. It is fine-grained and quite soft and porous.

The wrinkly skin

The runny type of lava called pahoehoe quickly forms a skin on its surface. This cools first. The lava underneath is still moving and causes the skin to fold and wrinkle. In large flows the surface may cool to form a solid crust, while lava still runs underneath.

Ropy lava

The surface of pahoehoe lava often wrinkles up into shapes that look like bundles of rope. The picture shows this kind of lava, which is known as ropy lava. When a lava flow is thick, it also develops vertical cracks while it is cooling down.

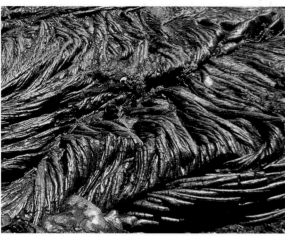

Sandy shores

In most parts of the world, the beaches are covered with pale yellow sand. But in volcanic regions, such as here in Costa Rica, the beaches have black sand. The sand has been formed by the action of the sea beating against dark volcanic rocks and grinding them into tiny particles.

BUBBLES AND INTRUSIONS

Rock slice
A highly magnified picture of a thin slice of the intrusive rock called andesite. When looked at through a microscope, it is possible to see the tiny crystals in this slice of rock.

IN the first project on this page we see how keeping a liquid under pressure stops gas from escaping. The liquid magma in volcanoes usually has a lot of gas dissolved in it. As it rises through the volcano, the pressure drops and the gases start to leak. They help push the magma up and out if the vent is clear. But if the vent is blocked, the gas pressure builds up and eventually causes the volcano to explode. The lava that comes from volcanoes with gassy magma forms rock riddled with vesicles (holes). The pasty lava from some explosive volcanoes sometimes contains so much gas that it forms a light, frothy rock that floats on water. We know this rock as pumice. When rising magma becomes trapped underground, it forces its way into gaps in the rocks and between the rock layers. This process is known as intrusion. The rocks that form when the magma cools and solidifies are called intrusive rocks. Granite is the most common intrusive rock. Often the heat of the intruding magma changes the surrounding rocks. They turn into what are called metamorphic (changed form) rocks, and are the third main rock type, after igneous and sedimentary.

DISSOLVED GAS

You will need: small jar with tight-fitting lid, bowl, jug, antacid tablets.

3 Now quickly unscrew the lid from the jar, and see what happens. The whole jar starts fizzing. Removing the lid releases the pressure, and the gas in the liquid bubbles out.

1 Stand the jar in the bowl. Pour cold water into the jar from the jug until it is nearly full to the top. Break up two antacid tablets and drop them into the jar.

2 Quickly screw the lid on the jar. Little bubbles will start to rise from the tablets but will soon stop. Pressure has built up in the jar and prevents any more gas escaping.

IGNEOUS INTRUSION

You will need: *plastic jar, bradawl (hole punch), pieces of broken tiles, modelling clay, tube of coloured toothpaste.*

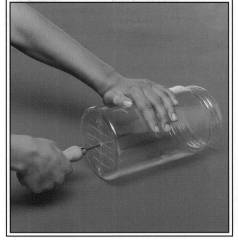

1 Make a hole in the bottom of the plastic jar with a bradawl, enough to fit the neck of the toothpaste tube in. Keep your steadying hand away from the sharp end of the bradawl.

2 Place the pieces of broken tiles on the bottom of the jar. Keep them as flat as possible. They are meant to represent the layers of rocks we find in the Earth's crust.

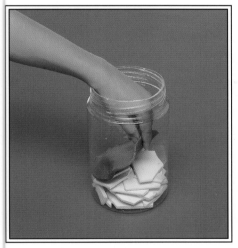

3 Flatten out the modelling clay into a disc as wide as the inside of the jar. Put the disc of modelling clay inside the jar. Push it down firmly on top of the tiles.

5 Squeeze the toothpaste tube. You will see the toothpaste pushing, or intruding, into the tile layers and making the disc on top rise. Molten magma often behaves in the same way. It intrudes into rock layers and makes the Earth's surface bulge.

4 Unscrew the top of the toothpaste tube. and force the neck into the hole you have made in the bottom of the bottle. You may have to widen it a little to get the neck in, but don't make it too wide.

VOLCANIC LANDSCAPES

THE landscapes in active or recently active volcanic regions are bare and often drably coloured. They do not look as if they could ever be covered with vegetation. However, they are not without beauty, and in time, plants will grow there. The constant action of wind, rain, heat and frost eventually breaks down the newly-formed rocks. The rocks turn into soil, in which wind-blown seeds soon germinate. Providing the climate is suitable, flowers, shrubs, and finally trees will eventually grow again. Sprinklings of ash from further eruptions may, in time, add to and increase the fertility of the soil. But there is always the danger that when a volcano erupts it will destroy all the plants that have grown since the last eruption. This can happen in hours. After the enormous eruption of Mount St Helens in 1980, the blast, hot ash cloud and mud avalanches killed everything within 25km. Less than a month afterwards, however, wildflowers began to grow, and soon insects and small animals began returning.

Blooms in a cinder desert
Hot cinders once blanketed the ground here. Since then wind-blown seeds have settled, germinated, grown into plants, and flowered. Their roots will help break down the cinders into better soil.

Dead landscape
A typical volcanic landscape in Iceland looks bleak before regeneration. Volcanic peaks tower in the distance, while in the foreground are bare, black volcanic rocks. Winter is coming, and temperatures are struggling to rise above freezing point. Conditions do not seem favourable for plant life.

Suitable soil
Here in another part of Iceland, the ground is carpeted with low-growing plants. They are growing in the thin soil that now covers a former lava field. The action of the weather and primitive plants such as mosses and lichens have broken down the lava into soil deep enough to support larger plants.

Etna's attractions

Giant cinder cones known as the Silvestri craters are on the southern side of Mount Etna in Sicily. The 3,390m-high mountain erupts frequently. It is one of a string of volcanoes in the Mediterranean region. The others include Stromboli, Vulcano and, most famously, Vesuvius. Geologists estimate that Mount Etna has probably been active for more than 2.5 million years. More than 110 eruptions of the volcano have been recorded since 1500BC. A particularly long eruption in 1992 destroyed much farmland and threatened several villages. The city of Catania, on the lower slopes of the mountain, is often showered with ash.

Rich paddies

Terraces of paddy fields are built on the slopes of hillsides in Bali in Indonesia, south-east Asia. The soil is very fertile because of the ash blasted out by the many volcanoes on the island. Terracing helps increase the amount of farming land and conserves water. In the hot, humid conditions, farmers can grow several crops of rice every year.

Fruit of the vine

Grape vines grow in vineyards on fertile land on the Italian island of Sicily. The land has been fertilized for centuries by the ash from regular eruptions of the island's famous volcano Mount Etna, which looms menacingly on the skyline. Etna is Europe's most active volcano.

Unstoppable

Nothing can stop this thick ribbon of lava, from an erupting volcano named Kimanura, smashing its way through tropical forest in Zaire. There are a number of active volcanoes along Zaire's eastern border. The border is in the Great Rift Valley, where plates meet, causing volcanic activity.

LETTING OFF STEAM

Hothouses
Here in Iceland, the greenhouses are heated by hot water piped in from the many hot springs in the rocks. The people of Iceland rely more on geothermal heating than any other nation.

THE molten rock, or magma, in the earth's mantle does not always break out to create volcanoes. Sometimes it stays beneath the Earth's crust. There it causes other volcanic features. They are called geothermal features because they are almost always caused by the Earth (geo) creating heat (thermal) in underground magma that then affects underground water. The most spectacular geothermal feature is the geyser. This is a fountain of steam and water that erupts from holes in the ground. Vents (holes) called fumaroles, where steam escapes gently, are more common. They may also give out carbon dioxide and sulphurous fumes. Also common are hot springs, where water becomes heated in underground rocks to a temperature above body heat (about 37°C). Some hot springs can be twice this hot. Many are rich in minerals. For centuries people have believed that bathing in these mineral-rich springs is good for health.

Iceland *geysir*
A column of steam and water spurts out of the ground and high into the air as Iceland's Strokkur geyser erupts. It is just one of hundreds of geysers found in Iceland. The word geyser comes from the Icelandic word *geysir* (upwards force). Geysers may erupt every few days or hours. Some erupt at such exactly regular intervals that people can set their watches by them.

Boiling tar
In a volcanically active region in New Zealand, geothermal heating is causing this tarpit to boil and bubble. New Zealand was one of the first countries to tap geothermal energy for power production.

Hot dip

Icelanders enjoy the pleasures of a hot spring. There are hundreds of hot springs dotted around the island. The water from some of them is piped into towns to provide a cheap form of central heating for public buildings and homes. Geothermal heating has many advantages over conventional systems. It does not cause any pollution and will be available until the Earth cools in billions of years from now.

Yellowstone springs

A hot spring makes a colourful sight in Yellowstone National Park in Wyoming, USA. The intense blue of the clear water contrasts with the yellow and orange minerals that have been deposited by evaporation around the edges. Yellowstone is the foremost geothermal region in the USA.

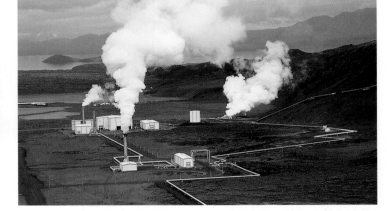

Gleaming terraces

Looking like a frozen waterfall, white terraces of travertine are found in many hot-spring regions, as here in Yellowstone National Park, USA. Travertine is made up of the mineral calcite.

Steam power

A geothermal power station in Iceland makes use of natural geyser activity. Steam is piped up from underground and fed to turbogenerators to produce electricity.

FACT BOX

• One of the most famous geysers in the world is Old Faithful, in Yellowstone National Park in Wyoming, USA. This geyser erupts regularly about once every 45 minutes.

• Yellowstone National Park also boasts the tallest geyser in the world. Known as Steamboat, its spouting column has been known to reach a height of more than 115m.

GEYSERS AND MUDLARKS

ALL the different kinds of thermal (heat) activity that go on in volcanic regions have the same basic cause. Water on the Earth's surface trickles down through holes and cracks into underground rocks that have been heated by hot magma far below. The water becomes superheated to temperatures far above boiling point (100°C). It does not boil, however, because it is under huge pressure. Eventually, this very hot water may turn to steam and escape from a fumarole (vent where steam escapes). The hot water can also mix with cooler water to create a hot spring, or with mud to form a bubbling mud hole. Sometimes it turns into steam at the bottom of a column of water, creating a steam explosion that blasts water out of the ground as a geyser. The first project shows you how to make a geyser using air pressure to force out water. Blowing into the top of the bottle increases the air pressure there. This forces the coloured water out of the bottle through the long straw.

Waterspout
Superheated steam and water spout high into the air from the Lady Knox geyser at Waiotapu, in New Zealand. A cone of minerals has built up around the mouth of the geyser, which usually erupts for about an hour.

GEYSER ERUPTION

You will need: modelling clay, long bendy straws, jug, food colouring, large plastic bottle, large jar.

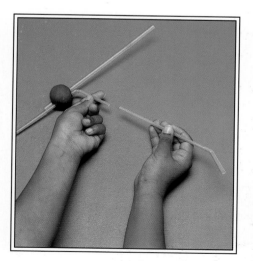

1 Make two holes in a little ball of clay and push two bendy straws through it as shown in the picture. Push another straw through the end of one of the first two straws.

2 Pour water into the jug and add the colouring. Then pour it into the bottle. Push the clay stopper into the neck so that the lengthened straw dips into the coloured water.

3 Place the jar under the other end of the lengthened straw and blow into the other straw. Water spurts out into the jar. If the long straw was upright, the water would spout upward like a geyser.

MUDBATHS

You will need: *cornflour, chocolate powder, measuring jug, mixing bowl, wooden spoon, milk, saucepan, oven mitt.*

1 Mix together two tablespoons of cornflour and two of chocolate powder in the bowl, using the spoon. Stir the mixture thoroughly until it is an even colour.

2 Pour about 300ml of milk into the saucepan, and heat it slowly on a hotplate. Keep the hotplate on a low setting to make sure the milk does not boil. Do not leave unattended.

4 Pour the creamy mixture into the hot milk in the saucepan, still keeping the hotplate on a low heat. Holding the handle of the saucepan with the oven mitt, stir constantly to prevent the thick liquid sticking to the bottom of the saucepan.

3 Add some cold milk, little by little, to the mixture of cornflour and chocolate in the bowl. Stir vigorously until the mixture has become a thick smooth cream.

6 Soon your hot liquid mud will start sending up thick bubbles, which will burst with gentle plopping sounds. This is exactly what happens in hot mud pools in volcanic areas.

5 If you have prepared your flour and chocolate mixture well, you will now have a smooth hot liquid looking something like liquid mud.

CHANGING CLIMATES

Mighty blast
In August 1883, the volcano Krakatoa blasted itself apart. The ash clouds from the volcano rose high into the atmosphere, spreading out and travelling in a band around the world.

VOLCANOES can have a noticeable effect on the weather locally (nearby) when they erupt. Over weeks or months, they can affect climates around the world. Locally, volcanoes can set off lightning flashes. These break out when static electricity builds up in the volcano's billowing ash clouds and then discharges like a gigantic electric spark. The ash clouds from volcanoes may be so thick that they block out the sunlight and turn day into night. This happened for hours in the region around Mount St Helens after the eruption in 1980. It also happened for days during the eruption of Mount Pinatubo in the Philippines in 1991. The Mount Pinatubo eruption also had longer-term effects. The gas and dust it gave out stayed in the atmosphere (air) for months, producing spectacular sunsets. So much escaped into the high atmosphere that it cut down the sunlight reaching the ground. This cooled down the Earth's climate enough to affect weather patterns for a number of years. The Mexican volcano El Chichon, which erupted in 1982, had the same effect. Its ash had a particularly high sulphur content. Chemicals containing sulphur are believed to block sunlight most.

A dying breed
The fossil skeleton of a pterosaur, a flying dinosaur that became extinct (died out) about 65 million years ago. It might have perished as a result of the Earth being plunged into darkness after planetwide volcanic eruptions.

Blowing its top
The crater at the top of the Mexican volcano El Chichon. Until April 1982 it had a jungle-covered conical summit. But on 4 April, this was blasted away in an explosion that drove ash high into the atmosphere.

Fissure eruptions

This series of volcanic cones follows a long fault in Iceland called the Skaftar fissure. Massive ash eruptions occurred along the fissure in 1783 and caused cold winters in Europe.

Chilly winters

The ash and gases from volcanoes can stay in the atmosphere for years. If enough volcanoes erupted at the same time, winters could be much colder than usual. In very cold winters in the 1800s, people held markets called frost fairs on deep-frozen rivers.

Red night delights

Spectacular sunsets often occur when eruptions throw dust and ash into the air. In 1991, before Australians saw sunsets like this following the eruption of Mount Pinatubo in the Philippines. Mud slides that followed the eruption killed more than 400 people.

Astronauts' eye view

Space shuttle astronauts took this picture of the ash cloud rising from the eruption of the volcano at Rabaul, New Guinea in 1994. It was estimated that the cloud rose between 20 and 30km into the sky. On the ground ash fell 75cm deep and destroyed two-thirds of the town of Rabaul.

FACT BOX

• The Indonesian volcano Tambora, which erupted in 1815, produced so much ash that world temperatures fell sharply in the following year. New England, in the eastern USA, had severe frosts in August.

• Mount Pinatubo, which erupted in the Philippines in June 1991, released nearly 8 cubic km of ash. This totals eight times as much ash as at the eruption of Mount St Helens.

OUT OF THIS WORLD

EARTH is not the only place in the universe that has volcanic activity. Many other planets and moons in our Solar System have had volcanoes erupting on their surface at some time in their history. Two of the planets nearest to us, Venus and Mars, were affected by volcanoes. Venus and Mars are both terrestrial (Earth-like) planets, with a similar rocky structure to Earth. The whole landscape of Venus, revealed by the Magellan radar probe between 1990 and 1994, is volcanic. There are volcanoes everywhere. Most of the surface consists of vast lava plains stretching for thousands of kilometres. Mars has fewer volcanoes, but they are gigantic. The record-breaker is Olympus Mons, which is more than five times the height of Earth's highest mountain, Mount Everest. Nearer home, volcanoes have been a major force in shaping our Moon. The dark patches we see on the Moon at night are flat plains that flooded with lava when massive volcanic eruptions took place long ago. But some of the most interesting volcanoes lie much farther away, on one of Jupiter's moons, Io. Its volcanoes pour out liquid sulphur.

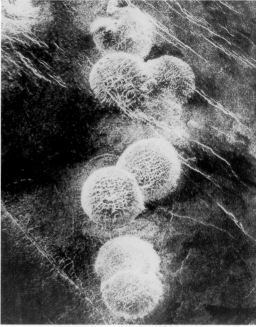

Volcanic pancakes
A series of volcanic features on Venus are called pancake domes. Scientists think they form when molten rock pours out of flat ground, spreads out and hardens.

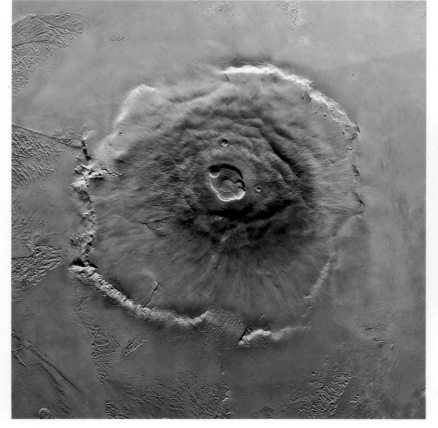

The greatest
This is the biggest volcano on Mars, and one of the biggest we know in the whole Solar System. It is named Olympus Mons, or Mount Olympus. The volcano is 600km across at the base, and it rises to a height of some 27km.

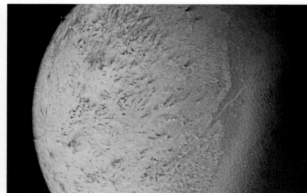

Triton's eruptions
Volcanic eruptions take place on Triton, the largest moon of Neptune. Because the moon is very cold (about −235°C), its volcanoes give off liquid nitrogen. Dark material comes out as well, causing the dark streaks visible in the picture.

Out on a limb

A volcano erupts on the edge, or limb, of Jupiter's moon Io. It shoots gas and dust hundreds of kilometres into space as well as pouring molten material over Io's surface. The material that comes out of the volcano is not molten rock, however. It is a liquid form of the chemical sulphur. Sulphur is a yellow-orange colour, which explains why Io is such a colourful moon. Io's volcanoes were among the many astonishing discoveries made by the Voyager space probes. They visited the outer planets between 1979 and 1989.

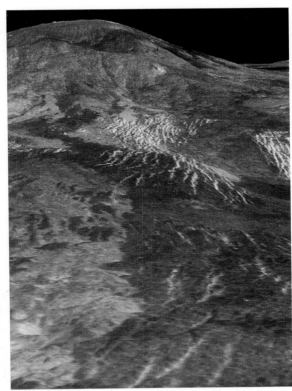

Volcano on Venus

One of Venus's many volcanoes recorded by the Magellan space probe. It has the typical broad dome shape of the shield volcanoes on Earth. Most volcanoes on Venus are of this type and, like all shield-type volcanoes, they pour out runny lava. Repeated eruptions over millions of years have sent rivers of lava streaming for hundreds of kilometres around. Most of the landscape of Venus consists of rolling plains made up of such lava flows. Venus's biggest volcanoes are up to 500km across and several kilometres high, but most are much smaller. Venus has many other volcanic features, including strange, spidery structures called arachnoids.

The lunar seas

The seas on the Moon are flat plains. They were created billions of years ago when lava flooded into huge craters made by meteorites. The picture shows part of the Moon's largest sea, which is called the Ocean of Storms. This sea covers more than 5 million sq km, and is more than half as big again as the Mediterranean Sea on Earth. The large crater in the picture is called Kepler by astronomers. It is about 35km from one side to the other.

THE QUAKING EARTH

Famous fault
The most famous earthquake-producing fault in the world is the San Andreas in California, USA. It runs for hundreds of kilometres, passing close to the cities of Los Angeles and San Francisco.

Many people consider the city of San Francisco, in California, to be one of the most beautiful in the world. It has a stunning setting on the USA's west coast and enjoys a pleasant climate. But living in the city has one major disadvantage. San Francisco sits nearly on top of a line of weakness in the Earth's crust known as the San Andreas fault. The fault marks the boundary between two of the plates in the Earth's crust, the eastern Pacific and the North American plates. These plates are trying to slide past each other. They do this jerkily and when they do, the ground shakes violently. Earthquakes occur around the boundaries of all the plates on the Earth's surface, especially where the plates are colliding. This is why they often occur in the same places as volcanoes, which also occur at plate boundaries. Tens of thousands of earthquakes take place every year throughout the world, but only about 1,000 of them are powerful enough to cause damage. Such earthquakes are incredibly destructive. Most only last for a few seconds, but in that short time they can reduce whole cities to rubble and kill thousands of people. The main earthquake is always followed by smaller ones. These are called aftershocks and happen when the rocks along the edge of the fault settle into their new positions. These aftershocks can also cause a lot of damage.

Not so grand
This old print shows the chaos and destruction that earthquakes can bring. This earthquake was in 1843, in the port of Pointe-à-Pitre on the island of Grande Terre. It is one of the Guadeloupe group of islands in the Caribbean.

Housing slump
An earthquake in San Francisco in October 1989 caused whole rows of houses to collapse or damaged them beyond repair. In only a few seconds, more than 60 people were killed.

FACT BOX

• The powerful earthquake that hit San Francisco on 18 April 1906 and the fire afterward destroyed the whole city. Almost 700 people died.

• It is estimated that as many as 750,000 people were killed in the Chinese city of Tangshan and surrounding regions by the earthquake there on 28 July 1976.

Anchorage in ruins
In March 1964, a powerful earthquake hit Anchorage, in Alaska. It was one of the longest ever recorded. The town and surrounding regions shook for four long minutes. Roads disappeared into the ground.

One-way street
An earthquake demolished one side of the Kalapana road in Hawaii in 1984. The ground was set shaking when the volcano Kilauea rumbled into life. Earthquakes occur frequently in volcanic regions.

No highway
In a 1994 earthquake that rocked Los Angeles, an elevated section of highway was shaken off its supporting piers (legs). Elevated roads are difficult to make earthquake-proof. The piers they stand on shake easily in earthquakes.

Kobe's killer waves
Some of the destruction caused by the powerful earthquake that struck the city of Kobe, Japan, in 1995. Multistorey apartment blocks collapsed like packs of cards. It was the country's most destructive earthquake since 1923.

SLIPS AND FAULTS

EVERY earthquake, from the slightest tremor you can hardly feel, to the violent shaking that destroys buildings, has the same basic cause. Two blocks of rock grind past each other along a fault line where the Earth has fractured (the crust has split). There are several kinds of fault. At the San Andreas fault in California, the blocks are sliding past each other horizontally. This is called a transform fault, or strike-slip fault. In a normal fault, the rocks are pulling apart and one block slides down the other. In a thrust fault, the blocks are pressing together, causing one to ride up above the other. Because the edges of the blocks in contact at a fault are very uneven, friction (resistance to movement) locks them together. As they try to move, the rocks become strained and stretched. In the end, the strain in the rocks grows so great that it overcomes the friction. The two blocks suddenly move apart. The energy in the rocks is released as earthquake waves that cause great destruction.

All shook up
Traffic lights fell over in Los Angeles, USA, after an earthquake in January 1994 which killed 60 people.

FAULT MOVEMENTS

You will need: two wooden blocks, jar of baby oil, drawing pins, sheets of sandpaper.

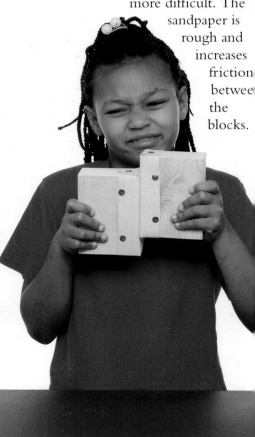

3 Pin sheets of sandpaper on the sides of the blocks, and try to make them slide now. You will find it much more difficult. The sandpaper is rough and increases friction between the blocks.

1 Hold a block in each hand so that the sides of the blocks are touching. Pushing gently, try to make the blocks slide past each other. You will find this quite easy.

2 Wet the sides of the blocks with the oil, and try to slide them again. You should find that it is easier. The oil has lessened the friction between the blocks.

QUAKES

You will need: *scissors, strong elastic band, ruler, plastic seed tray (without holes), piece of card, salt.*

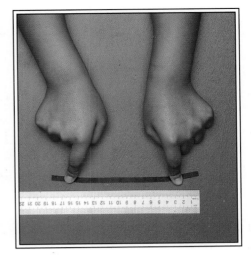

1 With the scissors, cut the elastic band at one end to make a long strip. This represents a layer of rock inside the Earth before it is affected by an earthquake.

2 Measure the strip of elastic with a ruler. This represents the original length of the rock in the ground. Make a note of how long the elastic is at this stage.

3 Stretch the elastic band and hold it over the tray. Rocks get stretched by pulling forces inside the Earth during an earthquake.

4 Ask a friend to hold the card on top of the elastic and sprinkle some salt on it. The salt layer now on the card represents the surface of the ground above the stretched rock layer.

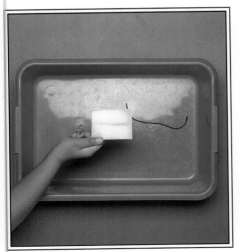

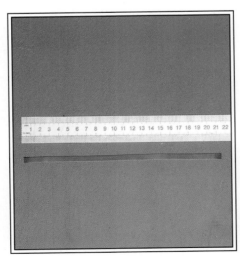

5 Now let go of the ends of the elastic. Notice how the salt grains on the card are thrown about. This was caused by the energy released when the elastic shrunk.

6 Finally, measure the strip of elastic again. You will find that it is slightly longer than it was at the start. Rocks are often permanently stretched a little after an earthquake.

No highway
Part of the elevated highway in Kobe that collapsed during the 1995 earthquake. The supporting columns were shaken into pieces by the force of the tremors.

TREMENDOUS TREMORS

THE movement of rocks that causes earthquakes usually occurs deep inside the Earth's crust. The exact point where the rocks start to break, or fracture, is known as the focus. This can lie as deep as hundreds of kilometres or as close as a few tens of kilometres. At the surface, the most violent disturbance occurs at a point directly above the focus, called the epicentre. The closer the focus, the more destructive is the earthquake. The earthquake that struck Kobe, Japan, in 1995 was so destructive because its focus was only about 15km deep. The focus of the great Alaskan earthquake of 1964 was not much deeper and caused massive destruction. The epicentre of that earthquake was on the coast of the Gulf of Alaska, and also caused the seabed to rise. This created a surge of water up to 21m high – it was a tidal wave, or tsunami. The tsunami devastated coastal towns and islands for hundreds of kilometres around.

Earthquake-proof
The Transamerica building in San Francisco is very distinctive. It has been built with flexible foundations. These should allow it to withstand the shaking that earthquakes bring.

struts hold pipeline above ground

Flexible pipe
The Transalaska Pipeline snakes through the wilderness of Alaska, carrying oil south from the oilfields of the North Slope. It is built above ground. There are zigzags in places to allow it to move if and when earthquakes occur. The pipeline stretches for some 1,285km.

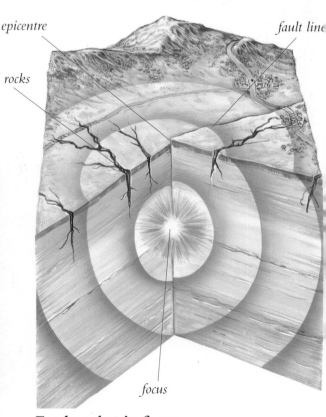

epicentre

fault line

cracked rocks

focus

Earthquakes in focus
Most earthquakes originate in rock layers many kilometres below the surface, at the focus. The most intense vibrations on the surface are felt immediately above the focus, at the epicentre.

Fire alarm

Fire breaks out in a gas main following a minor earthquake in Los Angeles. Underground pipelines carrying gas, oil or water are damaged easily when the ground vibrates. They can cause additional hazards to victims of the earthquake and their rescuers. The pipes break and their contents leak. Gas and oil catch fire easily. Water pipes can cause large floods.

Wall of water

This old print shows the tsunami (tidal wave) that followed the explosion of the volcano Krakatoa in 1883. Most of the people who died as a result of the eruption were drowned when this wall of water swept across the neighbouring low-lying islands.

Shipwrecked

One of the many fishing boats that were wrecked by the tidal wave that followed the powerful earthquake in Alaska in 1964. The wave devastated all the coastal communities around the Gulf of Alaska.

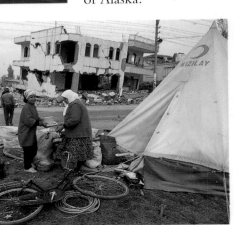

Displaced persons

Tents provide temporary shelter for the inhabitants of a town in nothern Turkey, following the earthquake in 1999. It is not yet safe to return home, even to houses that suffered little damage. A main earthquake is always followed by a number of aftershocks. If these are strong enough, they may bring down even more buildings.

The safest?

The designer of this odd-shaped building in Berkeley, California, boasts that it is the world's safest building. He claims that it can withstand the most powerful earthquakes. Berkeley is not far from the notorious San Andreas fault. It may not be long before we find out whether he is right or wrong about how safe his house is.

MAKING WAVES

Ripples in the street
The waves that travel through the surface rocks make the ground ripple. Afterwards, the ripples can often be seen. This road has been affected by waves in the ground. Now the surface of the road is like a wave.

T HE enormous energy released by an earthquake travels through the ground in the form of waves. Some waves are rather like water waves. They can literally make the ground ripple up and down. Others make the ground shake from side to side, which makes them very destructive. Waves also travel deep underground from an earthquake. The primary (P) waves travel fastest. They travel through rocks in the same way that sound travels through the air, as a series of pressure surges (pushing motions). The secondary (S) waves are slower than the P waves. They travel up and down and from side to side. They are rather like the wave you can see in a rope when you shake it up and down.

NEWTON'S CRADLE

You will need: large beads, lengths of wool, sticky tape, cane, four wooden blocks.

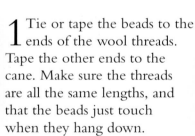

1 Tie or tape the beads to the ends of the wool threads. Tape the other ends to the cane. Make sure the threads are all the same lengths, and that the beads just touch when they hang down.

2 Prop up the cane at both ends on a pair of blocks supported by more blocks underneath. The blocks should be high enough to stop the beads from touching the table. Secure the ends with tape. Lift up the bead at one end of the row and let go. Look what happens to the other beads.

3 The beads in the middle do not move, but the one at the other end flies up. The energy of the falling bead at one end travels as a pressure wave through the middle ones. Then it reaches the bead at the other end and pushes it away.

TREMORS

You will need: *set of dominoes, card.*

1 This project investigates how the energy in waves varies with distance. Near the end of a table, build a simple house out of dominoes. Stand them up on edge.

2 Place the card on the dominoes to make the roof of your house. Many people in earthquake zones live in the simplest of houses, built not too differently from this one.

3 Go to the opposite end of the table and hit it with your hand, but not too hard. What happens to your domino house? Probably it shakes, but still stays standing.

Leaning tower blocks
After a major earthquake, buildings lean at all angles as the shock waves destroy their foundations. The 1995 Kobe earthquake in Japan damaged nearly 200,000 buildings.

5 Your house comes tumbling down. The waves you create when you hit the table are strong enough to knock down the house when it is nearby. When you hit the table from the opposite end, which is further away from the dominoes, the waves weaken as they travel. They are too weak to knock down the house by the time they reach it.

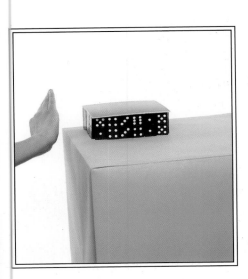

4 Now go back to the other end where your house is, and hit the table again with the same amount of force. What happens to your domino house this time?

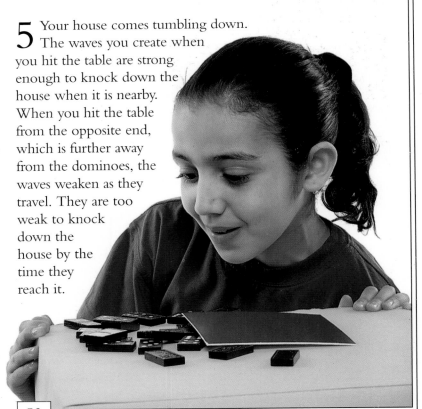

SEISMIC SCIENCE

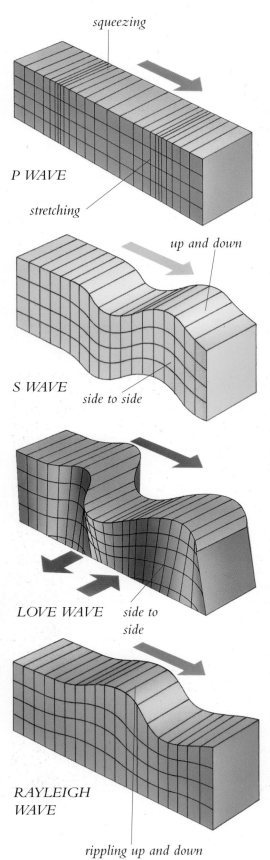

squeezing

P WAVE

stretching

up and down

S WAVE

side to side

LOVE WAVE   *side to side*

RAYLEIGH WAVE

rippling up and down

GEOLOGISTS who specialize in the study of earthquakes are called seismologists. These scientists call the waves that earthquakes create in the rocks seismic waves. The main instrument they use to detect and measure earthquakes is called a seismograph. Modern seismographs record the tremors (waves) an earthquake creates as a readout on a screen. The trace is known as a seismogram. It shows clearly the different waves earthquakes produce. The primary (P) waves, arrive first because they usually travel at speeds of more than 20,000km/h. The secondary (S) waves arrive next. They usually travel at only about half the speed of the P waves. Finally come the surface waves. Among other things, seismologists can tell from a seismograph how strong an earthquake is. The strength, or magnitude, of an earthquake is usually measured on the Richter scale, invented by Charles Richter. Other scales are also used, however, particularly one named after the Italian volcanologist Giuseppe Mercalli.

Making waves
This illustration shows four different ways in which earthquake waves travel through the ground. The primary (P) wave is a compression (squeezing) wave. It compresses, then stretches, rocks it passes through. The secondary (S) wave produces a side-to-side, shaking action. Love waves travel on the surface, making the ground move from side to side. Rayleigh waves are surface waves that move up and down. These two waves are named after the scientists who were the first to study them closely.

Charles Richter (1900–1985)
Charles F. Richter was a US seismologist. In 1931 he worked out a scale for measuring the relative strengths, or magnitudes, of earthquakes, based on the examination of seismograms.

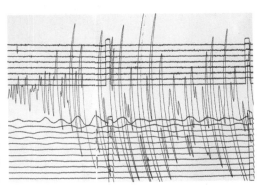

On Vesuvius

An Italian seismologist looks at an old seismograph at the observatory on Mount Vesuvius, near Naples. The building dates from 1845.

Bad vibrations

This is a seismogram of a moderate earthquake in California, USA, in 1989. The widest vibrations show the strongest earth tremors.

Looking for moonquakes

Apollo 11 astronaut Edwin Aldrin sets up instruments on the Moon in 1969. One was a seismometer, designed to measure moonquakes, or ground tremors on the Moon. Seismometers were set up at the other *Apollo* landing sites. They helped scientists work out the structure of the Moon.

Vibrating needle

A close-up picture shows the needle and drum of a seismograph. These machines are being replaced by electronic ones. They will be linked to computers that are able to record waves from earthquakes digitally.

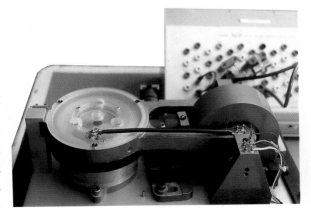

FACT BOX

• The work in the early 1900s of an Eastern European meteorologist (weather scientist) named Andrija Mohorovicic led to the discovery of the layered structure of the Earth.

• The United States National Earthquake Information Service is one of the key seismic centres in the world. It records around 60,000 seismic readings every month.

Round and round

A seismologist changes the paper roll on a seismograph at an Antarctic research station. There are many scientific observation stations in the Antarctic. People stay in them for months studying the Earth and weather.

BUILDING SEISMOGRAPHS

Out of a dragon's mouth
This is a model of a seismoscope built by a Chinese scientist of the past called Zhang Heng. The movement of an earthquake shakes a ball out of a dragon's mouth and into a toad's mouth below.

THERE are thousands of seismic centres scattered around the world. Within minutes of a quake, seismologists in different countries are analysing the seismograms from their seismographs. Then they will compare notes with scientists in other countries and will be able to pinpoint the epicentre and focus of the quake, its strength and how long it lasted. The Italian scientist Luigi Palmieri built the first seismograph in 1856. All seismographs work on the same principle. They use a heavy weight supported by a spring inside a frame. When an earthquake occurs, it shakes the instrument. The heavy weight tends to stay where it is because of its inertia (resistance to change). A pen attached to the weight records the shaking movement as a wavy line drawn on paper wrapped round a rotating drum. The same principle of the inertia of a heavy weight is used to detect tremors in the do-it-yourself seismograph shown in the project here.

BUILDING A SEISMOGRAPH

You will need: *cardboard box, bradawl (hole punch), sticky tape, modelling clay, pencil, felt-tip pen, string, piece of card.*

1 The cardboard box will become the frame of your seismograph. It needs to be made of quite stiff card. The open part of the box will be the front of your instrument.

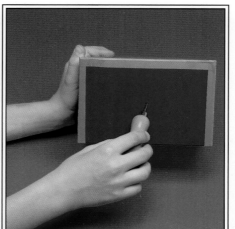

2 Make a hole in what will be the top of the frame with the bradawl (hole punch). If the box feels flimsy, strengthen it by taping round the corners as shown in the picture.

3 Roll a piece of clay into a ball and make a hole in it with the pencil. Now push the felt-tip pen through the clay so that it extends a little way beyond the hole.

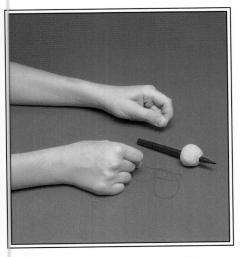

4 The pen and clay bob will be the pointer of your seismograph and make a record of earthquake vibrations. Tie one end of the piece of string to the top of the pen.

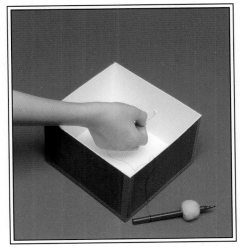

5 Thread the other end of the string through the hole in the top of the box. Now stand the box upright and pull the string through until the pen hangs free.

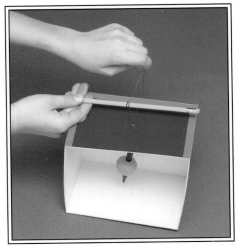

6 Tie the top end of the string to the pencil and roll the pencil to take up the slack. When the pen is at the right height (just touching the bottom) tape the pencil into position.

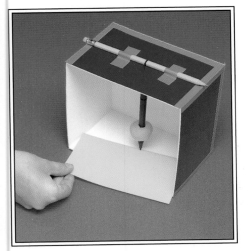

7 Place the card in the bottom of the box under the pen. If you have adjusted it properly the tip of the pen should just touch and mark the card.

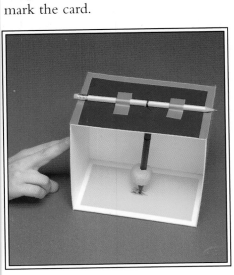

8 Your seismograph is now complete and ready for use. It uses the same principle as a proper seismograph. The heavy bob, or pendulum, will be less affected by shaking motions than the frame.

9 You do not have to wait for an earthquake to test your seismograph. Just shake or tilt the frame. The suspended pen does not move but it marks the piece of card, giving you your very own seismogram.

FIELDWORK

THE scientists who study volcanoes and earthquakes spend a great deal of time in the field (on the spot) around active volcanoes and in earthquake zones (places where earthquakes commonly take place). Volcanologists keep an eye on many active volcanoes all the time, looking for any changes that may signal a new eruption. Permanent observatories have been built on volcanoes near centres of population, such as Mount Vesuvius and Mount Etna in Italy. Hopefully the volcanologists can give advance warnings to people who could be at risk. When eruptions do take place, they chart the direction of lava flows and take temperatures and samples of lava and gases. The thermometers they use are not the mercury-in-glass kind. Those would melt at 1,000°C and at the greater temperatures found around volcano sites. Volcanologists use thermocouples to measure temperatures. These are made of metals. Seismologists spend their time in earthquake regions setting up and checking instruments that can record ground movements. This is part of their study to try and predict earthquakes.

Studying creep
A scientist measures movements along a fault using a creepmeter. The two parts of the creepmeter are on either side of the fault line.

Watching Etna
Mount Etna, in Italy, is the highest volcano in Europe. It has been erupting for more than 2.5 million years. Shown above is one of the three observatories set up on its slopes in the mid 1800s. The town of Catania lies on the slopes of Mount Etna. The volcano is watched constantly because if it erupts it could destroy Catania and other villages nearby. Fortunately eruptions on Etna happen quite slowly.

Hard-hat job
A geologist checks a lava flow from Hawaii's highly active volcano Kilauea. The sides have already cooled and solidified, which helps shield him from the heat given out by the river of molten rock beneath. He wears a hard hat to protect himself from falling debris.

Laser checking

Seismologists sometimes use a space satellite called Lageos to check for ground movements. Two identical lasers are set up, one on each side of a fault. Movement in the ground affects the time it takes for the laser beams to go to and from the satellite. These time differences tell the scientists the ground is moving.

Lageos satellite

Space age suits

These volcanologists look quite similar to astronauts in their protective suits. They are carrying out research in Ethiopia about the lava lake at Erta Ale volcano. The suits they wear have a shiny silvery coating. This reflects the heat from the hot lava away from their bodies and so helps to keep them cool. The researchers also wear protective helmets to shield their faces, particularly their eyes, from the heat. Erta Ale has been erupting since 1967.

On the ice

Geologists carry out seismic surveys in Antarctica to study the rock layers under the ice. In places the ice is more than 4,000m thick. Mount Erebus is the only volcano on the continent.

Thumping good idea

In the past, seismologists set off explosives to send shock waves they could measure through the rocks. Nowadays they mostly use special vibrator trucks, which thump the ground to create waves.

MEASURING MOVEMENTS

THE seismograph is the most important instrument for seismologists once an earthquake has happened. But these scientists use many other instruments, in particular to detect how the ground moves in areas where earthquakes might occur. The San Andreas fault in California is criss-crossed with seismic ground stations, some using laser beams and other electronic devices and others with relatively simple instruments. An extensometer measures stretching movements in the rocks. A magnetometer detects minute changes in the Earth's magnetism that often occurs when rocks move. A creepmeter measures movements along faults. Our two projects show how to make simple versions of instruments called the gravimeter and the tiltmeter. The gravimeter measures slight changes in gravity. When changes occur, the pull on a heavy mass changes, which will make a mass and a pointer attached to it move over a scale. The tiltmeter detects whether rock layers are tilting by comparing the water levels in two connected containers.

Seismic survey
Seismic researchers carry out an accurate survey of the ground in an earthquake region. By comparing their readings with past records, they can tell if any ground movements have taken place.

GRAVIMETER

You will need: *strip of sticky paper, pen, large jar, modelling clay, elastic band, toothpick, pencil.*

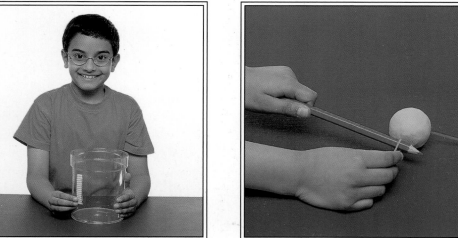

3 Lower the ball into the jar, dangling from the pencil, so that the tip of the pointer is close to the scale. Rest the pencil on the top of the jar and use bits of clay to stop it moving. If you move the jar up or down, the pointer moves down and up the scale.

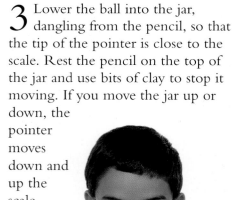

1 Draw a scale on a strip of sticky paper using a ruler and pen. Stick the scale on the jar. In a real instrument this would measure slight changes in gravity.

2 Bury one end of an elastic band in a ball of clay. Stick in a toothpick at right angles to the band to act as a pointer. Pass the pencil through the loop of the band.

TILTMETER

You will need: *bradawl (hole punch), two transparent plastic cups, transparent plastic tubing, modelling clay, pen, sticky paper, wooden board, adhesive, food colouring, jug.*

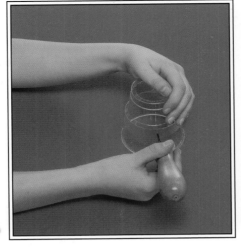

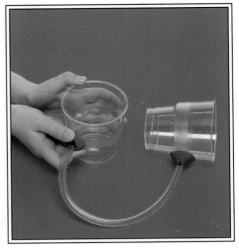

1 Use the bradawl (hole punch) to make a hole in the sides of each plastic cup, just about half-way down. Be careful not to prick your fingers. Ask an adult to help you if you prefer.

2 Push one end of the tubing into the hole in one of the cups. Seal it tight with modelling clay. Put the other end in the hole in the other cup and seal it also.

3 Using the pen, draw identical scales on two strips of the sticky paper. Use a ruler and mark regular spaces. Stick the scales at the same height on the side of the cups.

4 Stick the cups to the wooden baseboard with safe adhesive. Position them so that the tube between is pulled straight, but make sure it doesn't pull out.

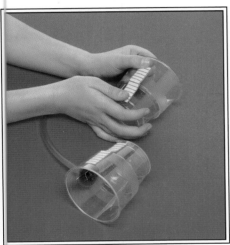

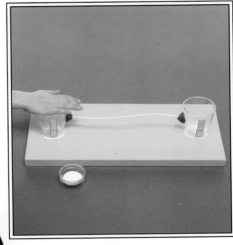

5 Add colouring to water in the jug, and pour into each of the cups. Make sure to fill them so that the water level reaches over the openings to the tubes.

tilt makes water flow out of upper cup

6 Your tiltmeter is now ready for use. When it is level, the water levels in the cups are the same. When it tilts, the water levels change as water runs through the tube from one cup to the other.

tilt makes water flow down into lower cup

TO THE RESCUE

WHEN volcanoes erupt and earthquakes strike, they can unleash destructive power equal to hundreds of atomic bombs. The most destructive volcanoes explode and cause ash and mud slides that sweep away everything in their path. Most people caught by these stand no chance and are dead by the time any rescuers can arrive. Earthquakes are even more deadly than volcanoes. They often kill thousands of people when their houses crumble about them in a few seconds. Many people survive the earthquake itself but are buried alive and often badly injured. It is then a fight against time to rescue them before they die of suffocation or their injuries. Many cities in earthquake zones have well-trained rescue teams. But when disaster strikes in remote villages it can be days before any teams can reach them. Often the roads to the villages have become impassable. All earthquake rescue work is hazardous. Aftershocks can bring down damaged buildings on the rescuers. Fire may break out from fractured gas pipes, and there may not be enough water for firefighting because of burst water mains. There can also be great danger of disease from the decaying bodies of possibly thousands of people and animals.

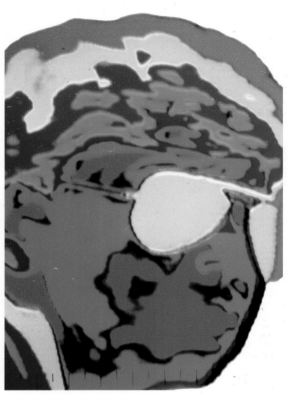

Body heat
This is a picture taken by a thermal imaging camera. It records heat, not light. Rescuers use these cameras when searching in dark places for earthquake survivors.

With bare hands
A survivor of the 1995 Kobe earthquake in Japan uses his bare hands to remove debris. He is searching for other members of his family who might be buried in the ruins.

Ash and mud
An aerial view of Plymouth, the capital of the Caribbean island of Montserrat, after the volcanic eruption of 1997. Thick ash and torrents of mud have covered the city.

Still alive
Rescuers have heard faint cries from the rubble of a collapsed block of houses. Carefully, they remove the broken concrete and steel girders and find a survivor.

Stretcher bearers
Four members of the skilled rescue team that battled with the devastation caused by the Kobe earthquake in Japan, achieve another success as they carry a survivor to safety.

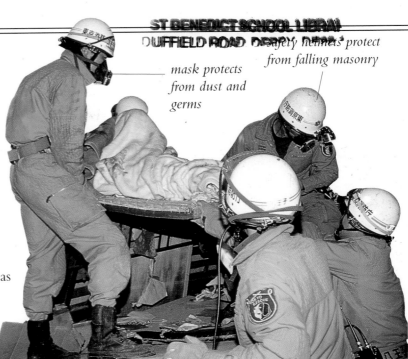

safety helmets protect from falling masonry

mask protects from dust and germs

Clearing up
Powerful excavators work round the clock to clear away shattered concrete and twisted metal supports from the collapsed Hanshin expressway after the Kobe earthquake in Japan. It took nearly a week to get the road back to normal.

Rescue man's best friend
Earthquake rescue teams not only rely on the latest scientific equipment to find survivors but also use sniffer dogs. Sniffer dogs are specially trained to use their sensitive noses to pick up the scent of people buried in collapsed buildings after an earthquake.

Heavy lifting
A crane is lowered to help lift the heavy steel and concrete beams of a collapsed building in Erzican, Turkey. These rescue workers are trying to free people buried during an earthquake there.

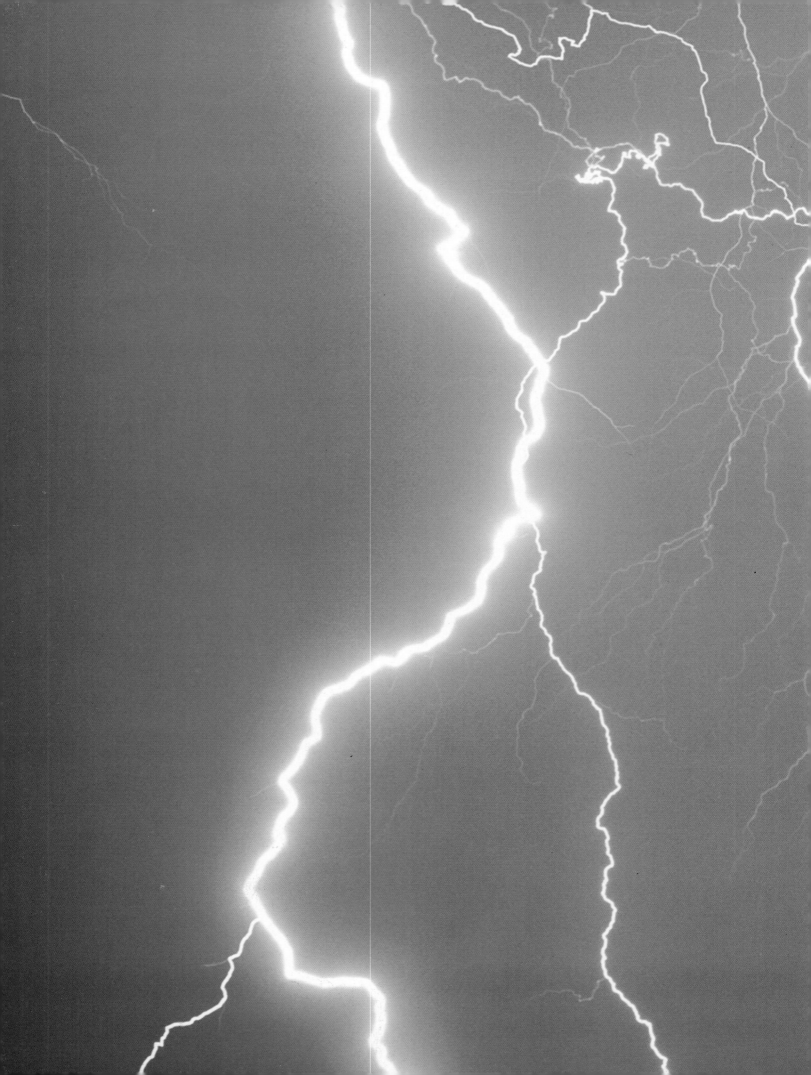

HURRICANES, TORNADOES & WILD WEATHER

WHAT IS WEATHER?

Some of the greatest challenges humans face are environmental disasters caused by the weather – from droughts and famines to blizzards and flash floods. Dealing with these conditions is an inevitable part of life on our planet. Sometimes the weather only affects our lives in a small way, such as in choosing what clothes to wear, or where to go on holiday. At other times, its consequences can be far more serious, as those who have seen the power of a tornado can testify.

Since the weather influences our lives in so many ways, scientists called meteorologists study patterns in the weather and try to forecast, or predict, what it is going to be like in the future. As research and technology advance, these predictions have become increasingly accurate.

Sense in the Sun
Many people find long, hot summer days a pleasant time of year, but the Sun can often burn your skin if you do not protect it. You should use suncream but, best of all, keep your skin covered up. Wear a sun hat to protect your head and sunglasses to cover your eyes.

Wrap up warm
Waterproof clothes, an umbrella and boots will protect you from the bad weather in most countries. But some places, such as the Arctic, are so cold that exposure to the icy temperatures there may be life-threatening.

Snow fun
Many people enjoy playing in the snow during the winter. But a heavy snowfall accompanied by a strong wind causes blizzard conditions, which make the outdoors a very dangerous place to be.

Dry as dust
Death Valley in California, USA, is one of the hottest places in the world. Rain sometimes falls and collects into small pools. But the water soon evaporates, leaving the cracked ground seen here.

Water everywhere
Heavy rain has caused flooding in the town of Kaskakia in Illinois, USA. Local rivers have burst their banks, and many people's homes have been submerged.

Winding up
A satellite picture reveals a tropical storm developing in the middle of the Pacific Ocean. Clouds spiral around the centre of an area of low pressure, driven by winds that may reach speeds of up to 200km/h.

Terror twister
A tornado powers its way through a small town in Texas, USA. The rapidly swirling winds of a tornado, or twister, can devastate buildings, uproot trees and toss vehicles into the air, cutting a path of destruction.

HEAT FROM THE SUN

Sun worship
An ancient Egyptian relief carved from limestone shows the pharaoh Akhenaten. He is offering sacred lotus flowers to the Sun god, Aten. The ancient Egyptian people worshipped the Sun god because they recognized that life depended on the Sun. They kept track of time by watching the Sun rise and fall in the sky, and they realized that their crops depended on the Sun to survive.

THE Sun is a gigantic star that pours out vast amounts of energy, called electromagnetic radiation, into space. Although just a tiny amount of this energy reaches the Earth, it is enough to make rocks so hot that eggs can be fried on them. This heat energy also stirs the atmosphere into motion, powering the Earth's different weather systems.

Different parts of the Earth receive different amounts of heat from the Sun. The lower the Sun is in the sky, the less heat it provides. The Sun is directly overhead at the Equator, so it is much warmer here than at the Earth's poles. Some of the Sun's energy is reflected by the Earth's clouds, some by the ground and some by the atmosphere. The amount of heat that any one place receives from the Sun also changes from season to season.

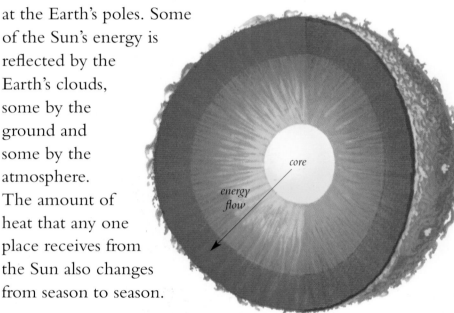

core

energy flow

Hot stuff
The Sun's energy is produced in its centre, called the core, where the temperature reaches 15,000,000°C. At this temperature, gases fuse (combine) to produce vast amounts of energy in the form of electromagnetic radiation, most of which is released as heat and light.

Heating the Earth
The Sun pours energy on to the Earth as heat and light. Some bounces off a thin blanket of gases, known as the atmosphere, back into space. The rest heats up the oceans, land and air. At night, clouds in the atmosphere help to stop heat escaping back into space.

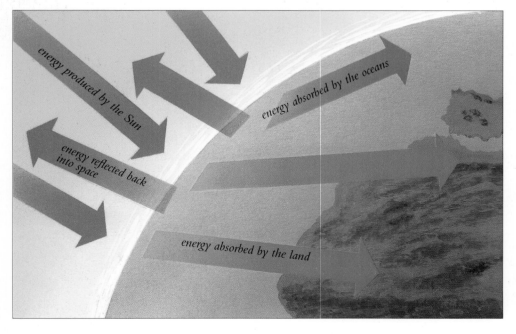

energy produced by the Sun

energy absorbed by the oceans

energy reflected back into space

energy absorbed by the land

Snowy December

During the winter in New York City, USA, it often snows in December and it is bitterly cold. The temperature may be just above freezing point (0°C), and a biting cold wind will make it feel even colder. New York is in the Northern Hemisphere. In this part of the world, the colder winter months begin around December. This is the time of year when the Northern Hemisphere is tilted most away from the Sun.

March

Earth's orbit

June

Sun

September

December

The changing seasons

Any one place on the Earth does not always receive the same amount of energy from the Sun. In fact, it changes with the seasons. Most energy is received in the summer season and least in the winter season. The seasons change because the Earth's axis is tilted in space. In summer, one half, or hemisphere, tilts towards the Sun and is warmer. In winter, the hemisphere tilts away from the Sun, and it is colder here.

Harnessing the Sun

A huge solar power plant in California, USA, converts energy from the Sun into electrical energy. Giant mirrors reflect sunlight on to a tank of water at the top of the tower. The water gets hot and boils, creating steam which drives giant turbines that generate the electricity. Solar power plants are useful in warm climates where the Sun shines steadily for most of the time.

Sunny December

In December, temperatures can exceed 30°C on beaches in Australia. Australia is in the Southern Hemisphere, where seasons are opposite to those in the Northern Hemisphere.

MEASURING TEMPERATURE

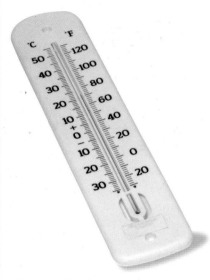

WHAT we notice most about the weather is the temperature – that is, how hot or cold it is. Temperature is measured using a thermometer. There are many different types of thermometer, but the most common consists of a glass column partially filled with a liquid such as alcohol or mercury (a liquid metal). When the temperature increases, the liquid expands in proportion to the rise in temperature and increases in length up the glass column. Similarly, a decrease in temperature causes the liquid in the glass column to decrease in length. This means that thermometers can record a range of temperatures. The simple thermometer in the experiment is made using water and can be used to record changes in temperature.

A simple thermometer
The temperature of the air can be measured using a simple mercury thermometer. Most have two temperature scales: degrees Celsius (°C) and degrees Fahrenheit (°F).

FACT BOX

• The human body is normally a constant temperature of 37°C.

• In 1922, the air temperature in Al´Aziziyah, Libya, rose to a sweltering 58°C in the shade.

• Water freezes into solid ice when the temperature falls below 0°C.

• Some parts of the Northern Hemisphere experience winter temperatures that regularly fall below −50°C.

• At a temperature of −190°C, all the air present in our atmosphere would turn into a liquid.

• When low temperatures combine with strong winds, our surroundings feel a lot colder than the temperature alone would suggest. This effect is known as the "wind-chill factor". For example, a combination of a wind speed of 48km/h and a temperature of just 4°C produces a wind-chill factor of −11°C, although water will not freeze in these conditions.

Taking your temperature
A thin strip of heat-sensitive material, called a thermo-strip, can be used to record the temperature of the human body. If you press the thermo-strip against your forehead, the heat of your body makes the strip change colour. The body temperature of a healthy human should be about 37°C.

Highs and lows
A maximum-and-minimum thermometer is used to check a range of temperatures inside a greenhouse. This type of thermometer indicates the highest and lowest temperature in 24 hours. If the temperature drops below 0°C, the girl's tomato plant will die.

MAKE YOUR OWN THERMOMETER

You will need: *cold water, plastic bottle, food colouring, straw, reusable adhesive, piece of card, scissors, felt-tip pen.*

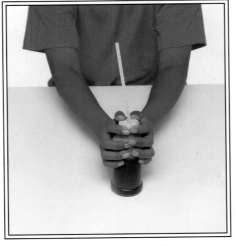

1 Pour cold water into the empty bottle until it is about two-thirds full. Add some food colouring. Dip the straw into the water and seal the neck tightly with reusable adhesive.

2 Blow into the straw to force extra air into the bottle. After a few seconds, the extra air pressure inside the bottle will force the water to move up inside the straw.

3 Cut two slots at either side of the card. Slide it over the straw. Leave the bottle to stand. Mark the card next to the water level to record the temperature of the room.

4 Then take your thermometer outside and leave it to stand for a while. On a hot day, the heat from the Sun will gradually make the air and water in the bottle expand. This will force water up the straw and past the level you marked for the room temperature. Mark the card again to show the temperature outside. Now put your thermometer in the refrigerator for two hours. The water level in the tube will drop below the room temperature mark. Make a note on your thermometer.

Stevenson screen

A meteorologist notes the temperature recorded by a pair of thermometers housed inside a shelter called a Stevenson screen. This protects the instruments from the weather. It is painted white to reflect sunlight and has louvred (slatted) sides to keep the air inside the shelter at the same temperature as the air outside.

CLIMATES OF THE WORLD

DIFFERENT parts of the world receive different amounts of heat from the Sun. As a result, they have a different weather pattern throughout the year. This changing pattern is called the climate. The world can be divided into regions with similar climates that suit different kinds of animals and plants.

In some regions near the Equator, the climate is hot all year round and plenty of rain also falls. Vast areas of tree-covered land, called rainforests, flourish there because of the heavy rainfall. On either side of the Equator, hot grasslands, called savannas, experience rain for only part of the year. Hot deserts are also found in this part of the world. Hardly any rain falls in deserts. Farther north and south, the climate is neither too hot nor too cold, and rain regularly falls. This is a warm temperate climate, common to most parts of the USA and Europe. However, the northernmost parts of North America, Europe and Asia have a cold temperate climate. The winters are long and cold, and plenty of snow falls. Evergreen forests dominate the landscape. In the far north of North America, Europe and Asia, it is too cold for trees to grow. These regions are called the tundra, and the temperatures may fall to −60°C. At the other end of the Earth, the continent of Antarctica has an equally cold climate.

Key to the climate
A world map can be divided into zones corresponding to the different types of weather patterns throughout the year. These are called climatic zones. Scientists classify climates in many different ways. The climate map below is divided into six different kinds of climate. Regions with different climates are inhabited by different types of animals and plants, which are well adapted to survive in their particular environments.

KEY

tundra
mountain
cold temperate
warm temperate
desert
tropical

Grazing the tundra
Caribou graze the thin vegetation of the Arctic tundra. The tundra has a harsh climate. In the winter it is extremely cold, and it only moderately improves in the summer. Most parts of the tundra are snowswept and frozen for up to nine months of the year.

In the tropics
Regions near the Equator have a tropical climate, which means it is very wet and warm. These conditions are ideal for rapid plant growth, creating rainforests. The trees and shrubs are evergreens, which means they keep their leaves all year long.

Arctic
tundra
conifer forest
deciduous forest

tropical forest

savanna

Mountain zones

Generally, the climate of a place is decided by its position on the Earth, but its altitude, or height above sea level, is also important. The temperature falls as you climb above sea level. Mountains in most parts of the world are layered with many zones, which have particular types of vegetation. These correspond with the climatic zones around the world.

Different types of mountains have different zonation. Generally, the Arctic zone is at the top, followed by tundra, then coniferous forest (evergreen trees with needle-shaped leaves), then deciduous forest (where the trees lose their leaves in winter). As the climate warms at lower levels, the vegetation becomes tropical forest, and finally savanna at the bottom.

An imaginary line called the snow line divides the Arctic and tundra zones. Above this line, there is a year-round cover of snow. Another imaginary line, called the tree line, divides the tundra and coniferous forest zones. Above this line, trees do not grow.

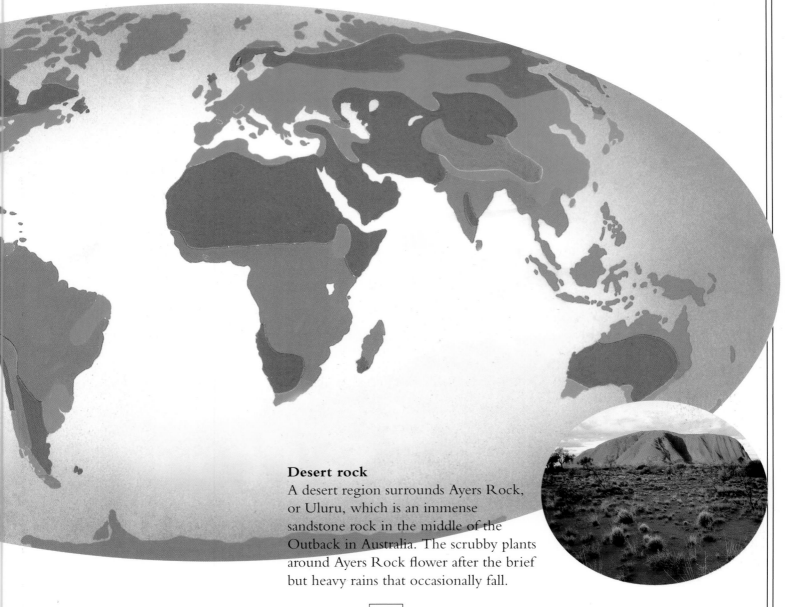

Desert rock

A desert region surrounds Ayers Rock, or Uluru, which is an immense sandstone rock in the middle of the Outback in Australia. The scrubby plants around Ayers Rock flower after the brief but heavy rains that occasionally fall.

73

CHANGING THE TEMPERATURE

Cool colour

In hot places, such as this town in Spain, all the houses are whitewashed to reflect the sunlight and keep people cool. There is not a dark house to be seen, because dark houses warm up faster by day and cool down faster at night.

DARK AND LIGHT

You will need: *two identical glass jars with lids (paint the outside of one black and the other white), sand, watch, thermometer, notebook, pen.*

THE TEMPERATURE of a place is controlled by different factors. The main factor is the amount of energy a place absorbs from the Sun, but other conditions play a part in controlling temperature, too. For instance, areas at very high altitudes are much colder than areas at sea level. Another factor is distance of a place from the sea. This is because the continents and the oceans do not heat up and cool down in the same way as each other. Water takes longer to heat up than the land, but the water holds its heat for much longer. Therefore, summers are cooler and winters are milder on the coast than they are inland.

Since water can circulate, it can move the heat from place to place in the form of ocean currents. Ocean currents therefore often affect air temperatures. For example, Britain and Labrador in Canada are the same distance from the Equator (they are the same latitude) but have very different climates. This is because a vast water current, called the Gulf Stream, transports warm water from the distant Gulf of Mexico to western Europe. This helps to keep winter temperatures much warmer in Britain than they are in Labrador.

1 Fill the two painted jars with sand to about the same level. Screw the lids on firmly. Place both jars outside in the sunlight and leave them there for about two hours.

2 Now take the temperature of the sand in each jar. The sand in the black jar will be hotter than the sand in the white jar. Write down the temperatures in your notebook.

3 Now put the jars in the shade. Note the temperature of the sand in each jar every 15 minutes. The sand in the black jar will cool down faster than the sand in the white jar.

MEASURING TEMPERATURE CHANGES

You will need: *two bowls, jug of water, sand, watch, thermometer, notebook, pen.*

1 Pour water into one bowl and sand into the other bowl. You do not need to measure the exact quantities of sand and water – just use roughly equal amounts.

2 Place the bowls side by side in a cool place. Leave them for a few hours. Then note the temperature of the sand and water. The temperature of each should be about the same.

5 In this experiment, the sand acts like land and the water acts like ocean. The sand gets hot quicker than the water, but the water holds its heat longer than the sand does.

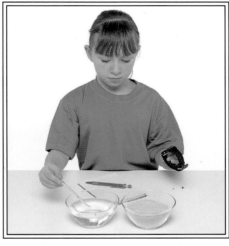

3 Then place the bowls side by side in the sunlight. Leave the bowls for an hour or two. Then measure the temperatures of the sand and water in each bowl.

4 Then put each bowl in a cool place indoors. Record the temperature of the sand and water every 15 minutes. The sand cools down faster than the water.

Soaking up the Sun
Reptiles such as crocodiles are cold-blooded. They rely on the surrounding temperature to keep warm. Their dark-coloured skin helps them to absorb heat.

EL NIÑO AND LA NIÑA

GREAT masses of water are constantly on the move in all the world's oceans. They affect the climate of places along their path. For example, trade winds blow across the Pacific Ocean. Usually they are strong and blow from east to west. They drive a current of warm water westwards.

Every few years the trade winds suddenly weaken and the whole system goes into reverse. A warm ocean current, called El Niño (Spanish for boy child), appears along the coast of Peru. This reversal in direction of the ocean current has an alarming effect on the weather, causing heavy rain and flooding in some areas but drought and forest fires in others. After a while, the trade winds usually regain their former strength and things return to normal.

Sometimes, however, the trade winds become much stronger than usual and drive the warm Pacific Ocean current much farther west than usual. This reverses weather patterns, creating droughts in normally wet regions and floods in normally dry ones. This strong reverse current is known as La Niña (girl child). Both El Niños and La Niñas seem to be happening more regularly. Scientists are still trying to work out why this is so, but it could be caused by a gradual increase in the world's temperature, known as global warming.

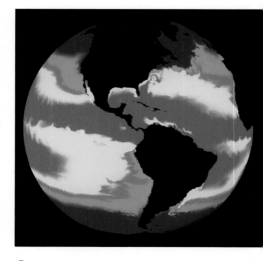

Ocean currents
A false-colour map shows how the temperature varies across the Earth's oceans. The warmest areas are red, followed by yellow, green and light blue. The dark blue areas near the North and South poles are the coolest areas. North and South America are the distinctive black shapes in the middle of the picture. The temperature of the oceans is due to the absorption of heat energy from the Sun. As the waters heat up, they begin to move and form oceanic currents. These currents are partly responsible for the Earth's weather patterns.

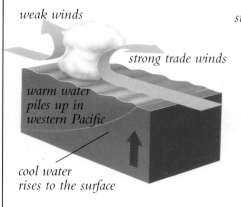

weak winds

strong trade winds

warm water piles up in western Pacific

cool water rises to the surface

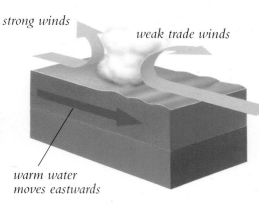

strong winds

weak trade winds

warm water moves eastwards

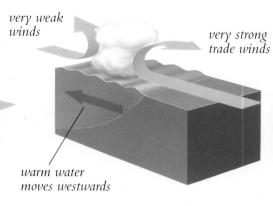

very weak winds

very strong trade winds

warm water moves westwards

Normal conditions
In normal years, the steady trade winds of the tropical regions near the Equator blow westwards across the Pacific Ocean. They pick up moisture from the warm oceans and deliver rain to countries along the western Pacific Ocean.

El Niño
During El Niño years, the trade winds blowing westwards across the Pacific Ocean become much weaker than usual. The warm surface waters of the Pacific Ocean are forced eastwards by strong winds, which carry stormy weather systems.

La Niña
During La Niña years, the trade winds blowing westwards become very strong indeed. The warm surface water of the Pacific Ocean is forced westwards, leading to storms and much heavier rainfall than usual around the western Pacific Ocean.

Stormy beach

Houses just inland from Huntingdon Beach near Los Angeles, California, in the USA, have been flooded by heavy rain. Precipitation (rainfall) levels in California are very much affected by El Niño years. The Californian coast is normally dry and sunny. El Niño may cause a vast increase in precipitation but may also give rise to drought here. The El Niño of 1982–3 was particularly destructive. The cost of the damage was estimated to be up to $13 billion.

Fire hazard

In 1998, forest fires raged out of control in Indonesia, in South-east Asia. Usually, tropical rains blanket the islands of South-east Asia, but El Niño was responsible for a huge drought and subsequent forest fires. More than 20,000sq km of forests were destroyed, creating clouds of smoke and haze that spread to neighbouring countries such as Malaysia.

Bringing flood

El Niño has caused widespread flooding in Khartoum, the capital of Sudan in eastern Africa. The climate of Sudan is hot with seasonal rains during normal years. In El Niño years, however, the seasonal rains can be exceptionally heavy, flooding huge areas of land and making tens of thousands of people homeless.

Bringing famine

In the El Niño of 1997 and 1998, flooding devastated the crops in Sudan. Millions of people faced starvation and were forced to leave their homes. As a result of the flooding, relief agencies supplied food aid in camps such as this one.

BEATING THE HEAT

WEATHER and climate affect human life in many ways. More people live in warm climates than in colder climates. In some places, long dry spells, especially when accompanied by high temperatures, can lead to a shortage of food and even widespread starvation. In fact, parts of Africa have been in the grip of major drought and famine for decades.

Humans have developed a number of ways to avoid the effects of hot climates. Loose, light clothes help air to circulate around the body and protect the skin from sunburn, which can cause skin cancer. In the Mediterranean and parts of Asia, the walls of houses are very thick, keeping the house cool in the day and warm at night. Windows are small and covered with blinds or shutters to keep out the Sun. The rooms are tall so that the hot air rises to the ceiling.

Animals and plants from hot regions have adapted over time to cope with their surroundings and survive the heat.

Water shortage
When the weather is hot, the body needs plenty of water to avoid dehydration. When the body becomes too hot, it produces moisture in the form of sweat, which then evaporates into the air. This cools the skin and the blood beneath it.

The goat herders
Yemeni women in traditional dress lead a herd of goats to drink from a water supply in the Arabian Desert. Their hats and clothing cover their bodies and faces and protect their skin from the Sun. If they become too hot, the rapid loss of water through sweating may lead to heat exhaustion. The symptoms of this include sickness, tiredness and fainting.

Saharan landscape
A Bedouin tribesman gazes out over the Sahara Desert in northern Africa, a region in which the temperature regularly exceeds 40°C. He wears loose, light-coloured clothing, which covers him from head to foot. The man's clothes allow the air to circulate around his body and also reflect the sunlight. This protects him from the Sun's relentless heat.

Keeping cool

Running in and out of the spray from a garden sprinkler is a fun way to keep cool on a hot summer's day. Droplets of water from the sprinkler collect on the body and take heat away from the body as they evaporate. This makes the temperature feel lower than it actually is.

Desert survival

The camel is well adapted to life in its desert home. Its most famous feature is its fatty hump, which acts as a store of energy. This enables it to survive for many days without food and up to ten months without water. The camel produces very little urine, which cuts down water loss. The animal's thick fur also keeps it warm during the cold desert nights.

No sweat

The elephant's natural habitats are Africa and Asia. Its wrinkled and hairless skin retains water to help the animal cool down. The elephant does not sweat, but it can flap its two large ears to lose heat. The blood vessels in the ears are close to the surface of the skin and easily conduct heat away from the animal's body.

Prickly survivors

The huge trunk of the saguaro cactus is pleated like an accordion. After the rainy season, the stem absorbs water and the pleats unfold. A 6m-tall cactus can store up to a tonne of water in this way.

WHERE THE WEATHER IS

A lot of hot air
Hot-air balloons float quietly above the Masai Mara National Reserve in East Africa. A hot-air balloon is powered by a gas burner, which heats up the air inside the balloon. Warm air rises, so warming the air inside the balloon makes that rise too.

THE atmosphere is a layer of air that surrounds the Earth. Most of the air molecules are near the surface of the Earth. There are less air molecules the higher up you go, so the air is thinner there. At about 300km high, there are hardly any air molecules left in the atmosphere at all.

The Earth's weather mostly takes place in a layer of the atmosphere called the troposphere. This layer is between 10 and 16km thick. It is in this layer that clouds form, rain and snow fall and thunder and lightning take place.

In the next layer up of the atmosphere, known as the stratosphere, there is a layer of a gas called ozone. This blocks harmful radiation from the Sun. Recently, the ozone layer has been heavily damaged by harmful chemicals called pollutants, which include chlorofluorocarbons (CFCs). Despite a concerted worldwide effort to reduce their use, there is still deep concern that the ozone layer is thinning extremely rapidly. This thinning is especially noticeable over the North and South poles in spring.

Lights in the sky
Strange lights appear in the skies over the far north and far south, caused by particles from the Sun colliding with gases in the atmosphere. In the north they are called the northern lights or the aurora borealis. In the south they are called the southern lights or the aurora australis.

Into outer space
The region where the molecules of the Earth's atmosphere shoot off into space is sometimes referred to as the exosphere. This represents the upper limit of the Earth's atmosphere and occurs at around 450–500km above the surface of the planet.

Red sky

In the evening, the sky often turns red or orange. This happens because when the Sun is low in the sky, dust in the lower atmosphere scatters the blue light that we normally see. Only orange and red rays are left for us to see.

Blue sky

Skies appear blue because of the way light from the Sun is scattered by the molecules of gas in the air. Dust, water droplets and other particles reduce the intensity of the colours. The bluest skies are seen when the air is at its purest, away from pollution in the cities. Many people who live in cities travel out to the countryside to take part in sports and leisure pursuits, such as windsurfing. Cleaner air can help people to feel more refreshed.

Mountain high

The peaks of mountains often rise high above the clouds. At the top of a mountain, there are far fewer molecules of air in the atmosphere than at the bottom. The air is thin and lacks oxygen. This affects the functions of the human body, causing a condition known as altitude sickness. This may affect climbers and walkers at heights of around 3,500m and above. It causes feelings of sickness and light-headedness and, in severe cases, delusions or even death. This is the Aiguille Verte mountain in Chamonix, France, the peak of which is about 3,000m.

IN THE AIR

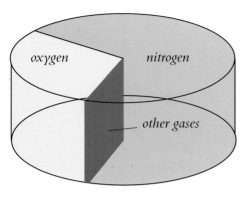

Gases in the air
About 78 per cent of the air is nitrogen and 21 per cent is oxygen The remaining 1 per cent is gases such as carbon dioxide and argon.

MEASURING THE OXYGEN

You will need: candle, clear mixing bowl, reusable adhesive, jug filled with coloured water, glass jar, felt-tip pen.

THE air we breathe is made up of a mixture of different gases. Nitrogen makes up most of the air's volume, but oxygen is the most important gas, because most living things need a constant supply of it to stay alive. We can work out the proportion of oxygen in the air in the simple experiment below. When things burn, they react with oxygen in the air and the oxygen is used up. As shown in the experiment below, if you burn a candle in a jar, you can use water to replace the oxygen that is used up. By noting how much water rises up the jar, you can estimate how much oxygen was in the jar to start with. You should find that the water level rises by about one-fifth, meaning that oxygen makes up about 20 per cent of the air.

Up, up and away
A gas called helium can be used to inflate balloons. Helium-filled balloons float away quickly if you let go of their strings, because helium is lighter than the air.

1 Secure the candle to the bottom of the mixing bowl with reusable adhesive. Pour enough coloured water in the bowl to fill it to a depth of about 2–3cm.

2 Ask an adult to light the candle. As soon as it starts to burn, place the jar over the candle. Let the jar rest in the water on the bottom of the bowl and watch what happens.

3 The water rises from the bowl up into the jar until the candle goes out. Mark the water level on the jar – this will show how much oxygen was in the jar to start with.

SEE THE WEIGHT

You will need: scissors, roll of sticky
tape, ruler, piece of thread,
two balloons of the same size.

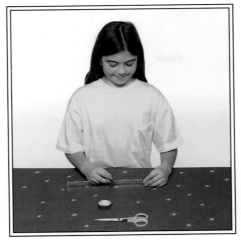

1 Using your scissors, carefully cut a small piece off the roll of sticky tape. Fix the tape around the middle of the ruler. Cut a piece of thread and tie it to the tape on the ruler.

2 Lift up the ruler by the thread and see if you can balance it horizontally. You will need to adjust the position of the thread until the ruler balances.

3 Take a balloon and blow it up a little. Take the other balloon and blow it up to a much larger size than the first. Carefully tape the balloons to opposite ends of the ruler.

4 Hold up the ruler with the thread. The large balloon makes the ruler dip down at one end. It is heavier than the small balloon, because it contains more air.

FACT BOX

• All gases weigh something, but some gases are heavier than others. For instance, hydrogen is lighter than helium.

• If our atmosphere consisted only of hydrogen gas, the balloon filled with helium would sink, rather than float away.

AIR ON THE MOVE

THE air in the atmosphere has weight. It pushes down on everything on the Earth with a force called atmospheric pressure. At sea level, atmospheric pressure is equivalent to the force of about 1kg on every square centimetre of the Earth's surface, but there are slight differences in atmospheric pressure from place to place. These differences make the air travel from a region of high pressure to a region of low pressure. This moving air is wind. Wind speed varies greatly, from a breeze (up to about 50km/h) up to a hurricane (up to 300km/h).

Breezes are gentle winds that often occur at the seaside where there is a difference in temperature between the sea and the land. The difference in temperature causes a difference in pressure and a breeze blows.

In contrast, large-scale wind systems blow all around the world, forming wind belts. These occur because of the differences in temperature between the hot Equator and the cold polar regions. The Earth is constantly rotating, and if this did not occur, the winds would blow from the high-pressure region over the cold poles to the low-pressure region near the Equator. Since the Earth rotates, however, this movement sets up a force called the Coriolis effect. This causes the wind to turn to the right of its path in the Northern Hemisphere and to the left of its path in the Southern Hemisphere. These two strong currents of air are called the trade winds, named because they once helped trading ships sail the oceans.

Sir Francis Beaufort
In 1805, English naval officer Sir Francis Beaufort (1774-1857) devised the scale that takes his name. The Beaufort scale soon became the standard method of estimating wind speeds, and it is still used today.

The Beaufort scale

The force, or strength, of the wind varies from place to place. The Beaufort scale is used to estimate the force of the wind. The scale is measured from Force 0, which means the air is not moving, to Force 12, which means a hurricane is blowing. One way you can guess the force of the wind is by the effect it has on you.

Force 0 on the Beaufort scale means that the wind speed is not noticeable. Smoke from a chimney rises vertically. When the wind reaches Force 2, you can feel the moving air on your face. This wind is called a breeze.

You can feel a Force 4 breeze pushing against your body when you walk.

| 0 | 1 | 2 | 3 | 4 | 5 |

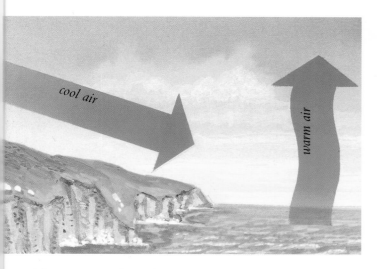

cool air

warm air

Land breezes and sea breezes

During the day, sea breezes are caused when the Sun heats up the land, and it becomes warmer than the sea. The warm air rises above the land, pulling in cool air from the sea. The opposite (shown above) happens during the night, when a land breeze blows off the land.

Go fly a kite

A young girl flies a kite at the seaside. A kite flies when air moves past it. The movement of the air produces an upwards force, called lift, on the kite. This force is responsible for supporting the weight of the kite and keeps it suspended in the air. The Chinese are thought to have invented the kite more than 2,300 years ago.

Wind power

Windmills were once used across Europe for milling (grinding) grain into flour. The enormous sails were powered by the wind. As the sails turned, they worked the machinery inside the mill.

Wind farm

Giant propellers harness the power of the wind at a wind farm in Altamont Pass in the USA. The propellers drive turbines that generate electricity for a nearby town.

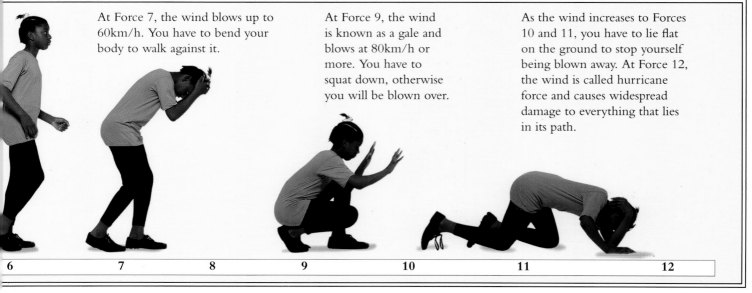

At Force 7, the wind blows up to 60km/h. You have to bend your body to walk against it.

At Force 9, the wind is known as a gale and blows at 80km/h or more. You have to squat down, otherwise you will be blown over.

As the wind increases to Forces 10 and 11, you have to lie flat on the ground to stop yourself being blown away. At Force 12, the wind is called hurricane force and causes widespread damage to everything that lies in its path.

| 6 | 7 | 8 | 9 | 10 | 11 | 12 |

AIR PRESSURE

THE weight of the air causes a force called air pressure to push down on the surface of the Earth. Air pressure causes air to move in the atmosphere, because the molecules in the air always move from areas of high pressure to areas of low pressure.

Air pressure varies according to many factors, such as air temperature and air density (how tightly its particles are packed together). The molecules in cold air move slower than the molecules in warm air and they crowd closer together. Dense cold air contains lots of molecules and puts a greater force on the Earth's surface.

Here are some tricks that involve air pressure. We can use the pressure of the air to knock a pile of books over. Sometimes paper can appear to be stronger than wood. This is due to the force of the air on the paper. In a fizzy chemical reaction, other gases, besides air, exert pressure on a balloon, forcing the balloon to expand.

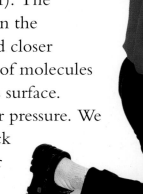

Pump it up
When you pump air into the tyres of a bicycle, you increase the number of air molecules in each tyre. The pressure of the air inside the tyre also increases – the tyre feels hard after you have pumped it up.

FEELING THE PRESSURE

You will need: *balloon, books, balloon pump, wooden strip, newspaper, thick protective glove.*

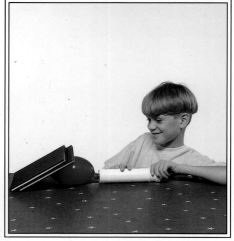

1 Place a balloon under some books. Blow air into the balloon using a balloon pump. As you pump, the air pressure inside the balloon rises. The increased force on the books pushes the pile over.

2 Cover the wooden strip with newspaper on a table. Leave a piece of the strip hanging over the end of the table. Wear a glove and strike the strip. Air pressure holds the paper in place and the wood snaps.

CREATE AIR PRESSURE

You will need: *funnel, bottle, vinegar, balloon, baking powder.*

1 Place the funnel in the neck of the bottle. Carefully pour in some of the vinegar, up to about half way. Make sure you wash the funnel after you have used it.

2 Fit the opening of the balloon around the bottom of the funnel. Carefully tip some of the baking powder into the funnel. Shake the powder into the balloon.

3 Carefully fit the opening of the balloon over the neck of the bottle of vinegar. Let the powder-filled part of the balloon hang down to one side of the bottle.

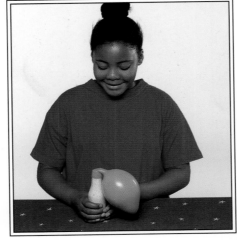

4 Gently turn the balloon over, so that the baking powder tips into the vinegar. The balloon expands as the mixture starts to fizz.

5 The fizzing indicates that a chemical reaction is taking place between the vinegar and the baking powder. This reaction produces lots of a gas called carbon dioxide. The pressure inside the balloon rises as more carbon dioxide molecules fill it. As a result, the increasing pressure of the carbon dioxide forces the balloon to expand.

WHIRLWINDS AND TORNADOES

Whirling wind
Dust devils spring up on dusty land in hot, dry summers. They pick up dirt and carry it high into the sky. The wind rotates relatively slowly in a dust devil, and so does little if any damage.

WHEN you see leaves spinning round and round in the breeze, you are witnessing a miniature whirlwind. A similar thing happens on dusty land in the summer. Little whirlwinds pick up the dry dust and spin it around and upwards into a spiralling column called a dust devil, which can climb up to 300m high.

Dust devils do little damage, but another kind of whirling wind is one of the most destructive forces in nature. It is the tornado, nicknamed twister because of its rapidly rotating winds. Tornadoes are born in violent thunderstorms. They form when a funnel-shaped column of whirling air forms beneath a thundercloud and descends to the ground. As it nears the ground, it picks up dust and debris. With winds racing round at speeds of up to 500km/h, a tornado destroys everything in its path, ripping houses to pieces and tossing cars into the air. A typical tornado is about 300m across and moves across the ground at a speed of about 50km/h.

Tornadoes occur regularly on the flat central plains of the USA, mostly along a broad path through Texas, Oklahoma, Kansas and Missouri. This area has become known as Tornado Alley. Tornadoes also form at sea, when they are called waterspouts. They are not as powerful and only last for only a few minutes.

A tornado is born
A huge thundercloud develops near Toronto, Canada. It is difficult to predict if a thunderstorm will give rise to a tornado, but meteorologists can tell where tornado-generating storms are most likely to form, and will issue a tornado warning.

Sinister silhouette
The setting sun highlights the dark shape of a tornado in Colorado, USA. The rapidly rotating column of air that touches the ground is known as the mesocyclone.

Fearful funnel

A dark, spinning funnel of a well-developed tornado heads for a town in Texas. If it hits the town, it will carve out a path of destruction several hundred metres across.

Furious freak

A freak tornado in Windsor Locks, Connecticut, USA, has left many houses in ruins. Tornadoes are most common in the Central Plains region of the USA. Here, severe thunderstorms often develop, and these are ideal for the development of tornadoes.

Watch the waterspout

Waterspouts are much like tornadoes, but they occur over water rather than the land. They are common in all equatorial oceans and inland seas. The water in the spout is formed by water vapour in the air condensing into water droplets. These are then pulled into the updraft within the cloud. Unlike tornadoes, however, waterspouts are usually rather weak storms and rarely cause much damage.

Tossed aside

Winds blowing at more than 300km/h have hurled an aircraft on to a nearby barn during a tornado in Louisiana, USA.

MEASURING THE WIND

THE wind shifts air from place to place and brings about changes in the weather. Meteorologists chart the direction and speed of the wind to help them predict these changes. They use an instrument called a weather vane to find out the wind direction. Weather vanes are often made in the shape of cockerels, when they are called weather cocks. The project on this page tells you how to make a simple weather vane.

To measure the wind speed, meteorologists use a device called an anemometer. Most consist of a circle of cups that spin round when the wind blows, rather like a windmill. The faster the wind blows, the faster the anemometer spins.

Going west
Weather vanes are commonly found on church steeples. This one points towards the east, which tells us that the wind is blowing from the east.

MAKE A WEATHER VANE

You will need: reusable adhesive, plastic pot and its lid, scissors, garden stick, plastic straws, coloured card, pen, sticky tape, pin, plywood, compass.

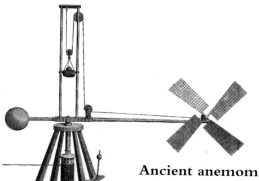

Ancient anemometer
The arm of this French anemometer from the 1600s moved when the wind blew against the propeller on the arm. The amount the arm moved was a measure of the wind speed.

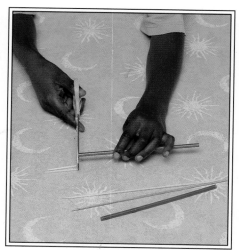

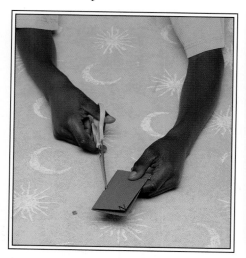

1 Stick a ball of reusable adhesive to the middle of the lid of the pot. Ask an adult to pierce a hole in the bottom of the pot with the scissors. Place the pot on to the lid.

2 Slide the stick into one straw. Trim the end of the stick so that it is a little shorter than the straw. Push the straw and stick through the hole in the pot and into the adhesive.

3 Cut out a square of card. Mark each corner with a point of the compass – N, S, E, W. Snip a hole in the middle of the card and carefully slip the card over the straw.

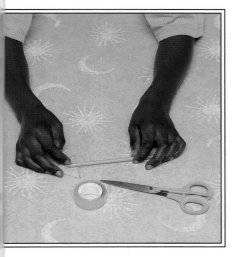

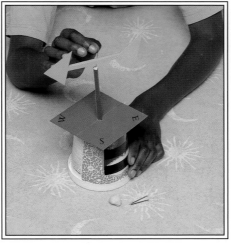

4 Cut out two card triangles. Stick them to each end of the second straw to form an arrow head and tail. Put a ball of reusable adhesive in the top of the first straw in the pot.

5 Push a pin through the middle of the arrow. Stick the pin into the reusable adhesive in the first straw. Be careful not to prick your finger when you handle the pin.

6 Secure your weather vane to a plywood base using a piece of reusable adhesive. Test it for use – the arrow should spin round freely when you blow on it.

7 When you have finished your weather vane, take it outside. Use a compass to make sure the corners of your weather vane point in the right directions. You can then use the weather vane to find out the direction the wind is blowing.

Windmills

The miniature windmills on the toy above spin faster the harder you blow on them. The sails of real windmills also spin faster as the speed of the wind increases. As a result, windmills need a "governor" to regulate the speed of their rotation so that the sails are not damaged in strong winds.

Wind direction

Don't forget that the arrow points in the direction that the wind is blowing from. So if it points west, the wind is a west wind.

HURRICANES AND CYCLONES

THE whirling storms we call tornadoes are extremely powerful, but they are only a few hundred metres across and travel only a few kilometres. Much larger and more destructive are the great whirling storms called tropical cyclones. They form over the oceans of tropical regions. Gradually, they grow into great spirals of dense clouds as much as 500km across, with winds whirling round at speeds up to 300km/h.

Tropical cyclones that form north of the Equator and in the oceans around the USA are called hurricanes. They are born in the warm waters of the Atlantic and East Pacific oceans and often affect the USA and the Caribbean. Elsewhere in the world, hurricanes have other names. For example, typhoons form in the North Pacific Ocean and affect Japan.

When hurricanes hit land, they unleash heavy rain and howling winds that cause massive destruction. Strangely, in the centre of a hurricane there is a calm area about 30km across, called the eye, where there is little wind or cloud.

In a spiral
Space shuttle astronauts photographed a cyclone in the eastern part of the Pacific Ocean, off California, that covered hundreds of square kilometres.

Hurricane Gilbert
Although the high winds of a hurricane can inflict a great deal of damage, the majority of destruction is usually brought about by huge tidal waves and flooding. In September 1988, a total of 200 people died when Hurricane Gilbert slammed the Gulf Coast of Mexico.

One in the eye

An image taken by the crew of a space shuttle in November 1991 shows the clearly defined eye of a cyclone known as Typhoon Yuri. This typhoon formed near the Philippines in the eastern Pacific Ocean. Gradually, Typhoon Yuri grew to be more than 1,700km in diameter. The clouds lining the wall of the typhoon extended to between 13km and 15km deep. A typhoon of this huge size would give rise to winds with speeds of more than 250km/h with sudden blasts (gusts) of over 270km/h – a truly awesome spectacle of nature.

Mitch's mudslides

Although the high winds of a hurricane can inflict a great deal of damage, it is usually the huge waves and associated flooding that cause the most damage. Heavy rain following the passage of Hurricane Mitch caused huge mudslides in Tegucigalpa, Honduras, in late October 1998. In total, 17 people were killed as a result of the mudslides alone.

Andrew the destroyer

Some of the 200,000 or more homes and businesses in southern Florida, USA, that were destroyed or severely damaged by Hurricane Andrew in August 1992. The hurricane left 65 people dead, over 160,000 homeless and caused about $30 billion in damages.

Path of devastation

A time-lapse satellite image of Hurricane Andrew shows the path it took across the Atlantic Ocean and across southern Florida, USA. The passage of the hurricane from right (23 August 1992), to middle (24 August 1992) and left (25 August 1992) was monitored by meteorologists. Warnings were issued but, although important, they are not always able to save lives and property.

THE WATER CYCLE

WATER moves around the Earth and its atmosphere in a continuous process called the water cycle. Heat from the Sun transforms water from oceans, lakes and rivers, into a gas, called water vapour, in a process called evaporation. In the atmosphere, water vapour rises, then cools and changes back into tiny droplets of liquid water. This is called condensation. Water droplets then gather together to form clouds. When water in the atmosphere is too heavy to be held in the air, it comes back to the Earth's surface as precipitation – dew, rain, sleet or snow.

On the surface, water can be consumed by animals or taken up by plants. Plants use as much water as they need and then release the rest back into the atmosphere in a process called transpiration. Sometimes water sinks below the Earth's surface to replenish underground supplies of water called groundwater. It can also remain on the surface in rivers and streams or lie frozen as glacial ice. Eventually, the water in lakes, rivers, streams and oceans evaporates once more to complete the water cycle.

Beneath the surface
When it rains, the water does not always flow into lakes, streams or oceans. Some disappears into the ground and becomes groundwater. In some places, this forms huge reservoirs of pure water hundreds of metres below the surface of the Earth. Underground caverns form in limestone rock by the erosion (wearing away) of the rock by groundwater.

precipitation

condensation

Sun

transpiration

evaporation

The water cycle
The Greek thinker Thales of Miletus (c.625–c.550BC) was the first to describe the water cycle, over 2,500 years ago. The four main stages are evaporation, transpiration, condensation and precipitation. They form a continuous cycle.

Elk in a fog

An elk looks lost in the early morning fog. When the visibility drops to less than 1km, the air is wet with tiny floating water droplets. This wet haze becomes a cloud resting near the surface of the Earth and is called fog. It is formed when warm air full of water vapour moves in above cold ground. The vapour then condenses into droplets of water.

City in a smog

A reddish brown smog smothers Hong Kong. Smog is caused mainly by the exhaust gases from the motor vehicles that clog the city's streets. These gases contain unburnt particles, which combine with a gas called ozone to form the hazy smog.

Mountain stream

A stream runs through a valley in the Rocky Mountains. On the horizon, puffy white clouds drift towards the high peaks. As the clouds pass over the mountain peak they develop into rain clouds. As the clouds pass down the other side of the mountain, they shed their water in the form of rain or snow. This will feed the stream with a constant supply of water.

Turning to vapour

Sunlight streams through a hole in a thick cloud off Maui Island in the Pacific Ocean. The Sun heats up water from the tropical ocean, and the water evaporates as a vapour in the air. As the vapour rises it cools and condenses, causing the cloud to grow.

HUMIDITY

WHY does 21°C in the Caribbean feel so much hotter than 21°C in Egypt? The answer is humidity – the air's water vapour content. When there is a lot of water vapour about, such as in the Caribbean, the air feels moist and sticky. This is because the perspiration on our skin cannot evaporate into the air very well – there is too much water in the air already. As a result, the perspiration stays on our skin and makes it wet, preventing us from cooling down. When there is little water vapour about, such as in Egypt, the air feels dry. The perspiration on our skin escapes into the air more easily.

Measuring the amount of water vapour in the air helps meteorologists forecast the weather. When the air is very humid, there is more chance that it will rain. Meteorologists use a device called a hygrometer to measure humidity. You could make a simple hygrometer using a long hair from your head. The length of hair changes as the humidity changes. This is the basis of an instrument called the hair hygrometer.

Another device meteorologists use to measure humidity is the wet-and-dry bulb thermometer, which contains two different thermometers. The difference in temperature between the two thermometers is used to calculate the humidity. You can make a simple hygrometer in this project.

Water producers
In the rainforests along the coast of northern California, USA, it is warm and humid most of the time. Rainforests contain thousands of plants, all of which give off vast amounts of water from their leaves.

MEASURE THE HUMIDITY

You will need: 2 sheets of coloured card, pen, scissors, glue, toothpick, used matchstick, straw, reusable adhesive, blotting paper, hole punch.

1 Cut out a card rectangle. Mark regular intervals along one side for a scale. Cut a 2cm slit in one short side. Split the parts out as shown above and glue them to a card base.

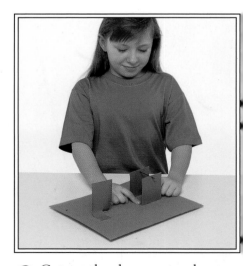

2 Cut another long rectangle from the first card. Fold it and stick it to the card base as shown above. Pierce the top carefully with a toothpick to form a pivot.

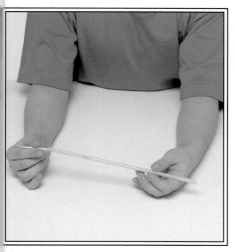

3 Fix the used matchstick to one end of the straw using some reusable adhesive to make a pointer. Both the matchstick and the adhesive give the pointer some weight.

4 Carefully cut out several squares of blotting paper. Use the hole punch to make a hole in the middle of each square. Slide the squares over the end of the pointer.

5 Now carefully pierce the toothpick pointer with the pivot. Position the pointer as shown above. Make sure the pointer can swing freely up and down.

6 Adjust the position of the toothpick so that it stays level. Take the hygrometer into the bathroom when you have a bath. The high humidity should make the blotting paper damp and the pointer will tip upwards. On a warm day outside, the blotting paper will dry and the pointer will tip down.

Transpiring plants

Plants play a vital role in the transfer of water from the atmosphere to the Earth. A plant's leaves give off water vapour in a process called transpiration. Cover a pot plant with a clear plastic bag, sealing the plastic around the pot with sticky tape. Put the plant in direct sunlight for two hours. Notice that the bag starts to mist up and droplets of water form on the inside. They form when the water vapour given off by the plant turns back to a liquid.

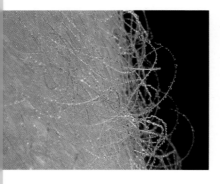

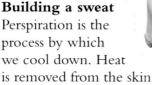

Building a sweat

Perspiration is the process by which we cool down. Heat is removed from the skin when water (sweat) evaporates from it. This process is less effective in humid weather when the sweat remains on our skin.

LOOKING AT CLOUDS

Without clouds, there would be no rain, snow, thunder or lightning and the sky would be very boring to look at. A cloud is a visible mass of tiny water droplets or ice crystals suspended in the air. Clouds can be thick or thin, big or little, and change form constantly.

They can be divided into four main types. Cumulus clouds are puffy masses that look like balls of cotton wool. Stratus clouds are flat and often cover the entire sky, extending many hundreds of square kilometres. Cirrus clouds are wispy and form up to 13km above the surface of the Earth. Dark clouds that bring rain are called nimbus. Cloud names can be combined. For example, cumulonimbus and nimbostratus are the names given to different clouds that produce rain.

Floating saucer
From a distance, this lenticular (lens-shaped) cloud looks rather like a flying saucer. These clouds often form in waves that develop downwind of a mountain range. Lenticular clouds are often elongated and usually have well-defined outlines. Frequently, they form one above the other like a stack of pancakes.

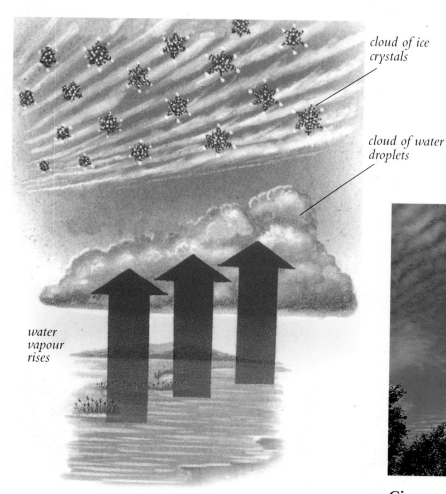

cloud of ice crystals

cloud of water droplets

water vapour rises

How clouds form
When warm humid air rises and cools, the vapour turns into droplets of water and forms clouds. If the air is very cold, the vapour will turn into a cloud of ice crystals.

Cirrocumulus clouds
The small ripples in cirrocumulus clouds look rather like the scales of a fish. The expression "mackerel sky" is used to describe a sky full of cirrocumulus clouds. These high white clouds are rounded and composed of ice crystals.

Cirrus clouds

The most common high clouds are the cirrus clouds, which are thin, wispy and made up of ice crystals. High winds can blow these clouds into long streamers called mares' tails.

Cumulus clouds

Puffy cumulus clouds take on a variety of shapes, but they most often look like balls of cotton wool. They have round tops and when they are dark and deep, they bring rain.

Cumulonimbus clouds

Cumulonimbus are thunder clouds. They are the largest clouds of all and form from cumulus clouds, often sprouting an anvil-shaped top, and produce heavy showers of precipitation.

cirrus

cirrostratus

cirrocumulus

altostratus

altocumulus

cumulonimbus

stratocumulus

cumulus

stratus

Clouds at different heights

Clouds can be grouped according to how high they are above the Earth's surface. High clouds include cirrus clouds. Altostratus and altocumulus are middle clouds. Stratus clouds are examples of low clouds.

The Sun's halo

A spectacular halo around the Sun is caused by a high cirrostratus cloud. Tiny ice particles in the cloud refract, or bend, light from the Sun to create a luminous ring.

RAIN AND DEW

IN some clouds, tiny water droplets remain suspended in the air. In other clouds, the droplets bump into one another and coalesce (join together). As the water droplets get larger and larger, they become too heavy to stay in the air. Eventually, the droplets fall out of the cloud as rain. Raindrops that reach the Earth's surface are rarely larger than 5mm across.

Rain is the commonest form of what meteorologists call precipitation. Precipitation is any form of water that falls from the atmosphere and reaches the ground. Dew is a form of precipitation. During a cold night, dew forms on surfaces such as leaves and the ground. The cold surfaces make the water vapour condense into droplets of liquid water.

From small beginnings
Rain falls from the dark base of a cumulonimbus cloud over the hills in the distance. Cumulonimbus clouds start as small, fluffy white cumulus clouds. Then they begin to grow and develop a dark base. Cumulus clouds sometimes mushroom into massive thunderclouds that reach up to 15km high and a severe thunderstorm may develop.

Walk in the rain
It is fun to go out in the rain but only if you dress properly. If you are wet, your body loses heat through the wet skin. If your body loses too much heat too quickly, a life-threatening condition called hypothermia may result.

A dewy web
Dew drops glisten on a spider's web. The dew formed on the web when water vapour in the air cooled during the night and condensed as water droplets.

Rain to come
Dark, stormy nimbus clouds are piling up in the sky near Majorca in the Mediterranean. The clouds are low and soon it will be raining hard.

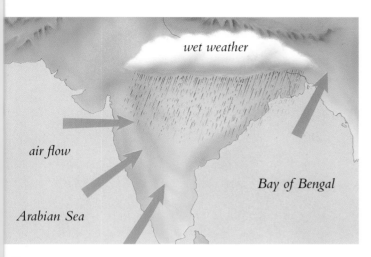

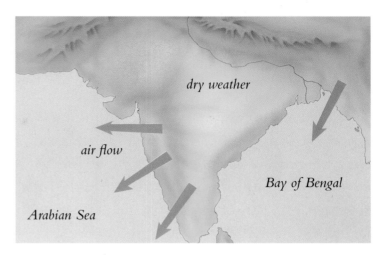

The summer monsoon

Some of the heaviest rain in the world falls in Asia during the monsoon period. During the summer, the air over the continent is warmer than the air over the water, and wind blows from the warm ocean. The winds bring heavy showers and thunderstorms, which can lead to flooding.

The winter monsoon

During the winter, the air over continental Asia becomes much colder than the air over the ocean. As a result, air flows out over the ocean. The winter monsoon provides southern Asia with generally fair weather and a dry season.

Railways into rivers

Days of almost continuous heavy summer monsoonal rains have turned this railway in Bangladesh into a river. The ground has become waterlogged, so the water will not drain away.

Moist air

In hot, tropical regions such as Hawaii, rain falls regularly throughout the year. Hawaii is surrounded by the Pacific Ocean. As a result, winds that blow from the sea to land bring air saturated (filled) with water vapour.

Summer burst

The monsoon rains fall across large areas of the tropics in summer, from northern Australia to the Caribbean. This monsoon rain is falling on a river in Indonesia.

MAKING RAINBOWS

RAINBOWS can often be seen during showery weather when the Sun is quite low in the sky. White sunlight is actually made up of a mixture of seven different colours – red, orange, yellow, green, blue, indigo and violet. Raindrops split up sunlight into a spread, or spectrum, of these separate colours to form a rainbow. The biggest rainbows form when the Sun is low in the sky, so they are most commonly seen in the evenings or mornings. They are also less common in the tropics, where the Sun is higher in the sky than in regions further north or south.

Other coloured effects can be seen in the sky. Sometimes a circle made up of faint rainbow colours, called a halo, forms around the Sun or the Moon. Ice crystals in front of the Sun or Moon split up the sunlight into a spectrum.

White light can be split up into a colourful rainbow spectrum by shining it through a prism (a triangular wedge of glass). In the experiment, you can produce your own rainbow by shining light through a "wedge" of water.

Midday rainbow
The mist of water created by waterfalls, such as Victoria Falls on the border of Zambia and Zimbabwe, creates the perfect conditions for the formation of rainbows.

Splitting up white
If you shine white light through a prism, it splits up into different colours and emerges from the other side as a rainbow – a coloured band called a spectrum.

Split into seven
Rainbows are made up of seven different colours: red, orange, yellow, green, blue, indigo and violet. Here you can see a double rainbow.

FACT BOX

• White light is not really white. In fact, it is made up of seven different colours, as shown above. These colours mix together to make white light.

• When light travels from air into water or glass (or back the other way) it is refracted, which means it bends. Different colours in the light bend more than others. Blue light bends most, red light least. As a result, the colours start to separate out and the result is a spectrum – the colours of the rainbow.

SPLIT LIGHT INTO A RAINBOW

You will need: *mirror, dish, reusable adhesive, jug of water, torch, piece of white card.*

1 Carefully lean the mirror against the side of the dish. Use two small pieces of reusable adhesive to stick either side of the mirror to the dish at an angle.

2 Pour water into the dish until it is about 4cm in depth. As you fill the dish a wedge-shaped volume of water is created alongside the mirror.

3 Switch on the torch. Shine the beam on to the surface of the water in front of the mirror. This should produce a spectrum or "rainbow".

4 It is best to do the next part of this experiment in dim light. Hold up the piece of white card above the dish to look at your rainbow. You may need to alter the positions of the card and torch light before you can see it properly.

THUNDER AND LIGHTNING

A THUNDERSTORM occurs when warm, humid air rises. The upward air movement may be due to the uneven ground or temperature below. Huge, dark cumulonimbus thunderclouds develop overhead, flashes of lightning may fill the sky and the ground often trembles with a booming sound wave called thunder.

Lightning is a huge discharge of electricity. In a thundercloud, tiny drops of water and ice carry little bits of electricity, called electrical charges, which build up in parts of the cloud. In time, this charge becomes so great that electricity jumps to the ground or to other clouds, creating great sparks of lightning. The lightning heats up the air to a high temperature and makes it suddenly expand. This creates the explosion we hear as thunder.

Mother of lightning
Sieou-wen-ing is a mythological character from ancient China. She is thought to be the mother of lightning. In this picture, she is sending bolts of lightning towards the Earth.

Ice block
Hailstones are pieces of ice that fall from clouds. This one is 15cm across. Most are much smaller, but they become bigger the longer they stay up in the clouds.

Flashes of lightning
Lightning illuminates the night above the distant mountains. Light travels so fast that we see a flash of lightning almost instantly. The sound of thunder takes much longer to reach our ears, however, because sound waves travel more slowly than light. Sometimes, lightning is seen but no thunder is heard. This happens because during a thunderstorm, the air moves erratically and often scatters the sound waves. As a result, the thunder cannot be heard.

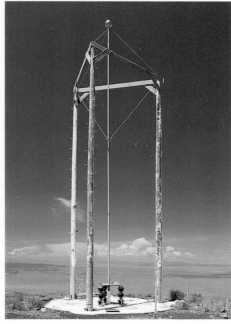

Lightning conductor

An experimental lightning conductor helps scientists study lightning. Electricity is easily conducted (passed along) through metal. Many tall buildings have a metal rod at the top. If lightning strikes, the metal conducts the electricity safely to the ground, and the building will not be damaged.

Struck by lightning

Lightning has struck a tree and left a trail of exposed wood in the bark. Lightning bolts often strike tall objects such as trees and buildings.

Bolt from the blue

A powerful streak of lightning discharges from thunderclouds and strikes a tree. The air surrounding lightning often rises to 30,000°C and may set the whole tree on fire.

CHARGING UP

THE lightning that flashes in the sky during a thunderstorm is not the same kind of electricity that makes your television or radio work. Lightning is a form of static electricity, which is made up of tiny electrical charges. These little bits of electricity can build up to create a much bigger charge, or voltage. Unlike ordinary electricity, the electrical charge does not usually flow away, which is why it is called static (not moving) electricity. In a thundercloud, the static electricity builds up so much that the air cannot hold it, and it jumps around as lightning flashes. In these experiments, you can build up small electrical charges by rubbing things together.

MAKE STATIC ELECTRICITY

You will need: balloons, balloon pump, hairbrush.

Van de Graaff generator
If you put your hands on a device called a Van de Graaff generator, your hair stands on end. A belt of material carries tiny electrical charges, which build up on a metal sphere, making static electricity.

1 Blow up a number of balloons with a balloon pump. Rub the balloons against a jumper or something made from wool. Put the balloons in different places.

2 Put the balloons on the ceiling, on the walls and even on your friends. The tiny electrical charges that form static electricity will make the balloons "stick" to things.

3 You can make your hair charge up with static electricity, too. Brush your hair when it is dry. Then hold the hairbrush near your hair. It will make your hair stand on end.

JUMPING ELECTRICITY

You will need: *plastic sheet, sticky tape, rubber gloves, metal dish, fork.*

Hands-on activity

If you put your hands over a plasma ball, little bolts of electrical charge move like lightning towards your hands. The "lightning" consists of harmless flashes of static electricity, travelling in a plasma (sea) of electrified particles.

1 Lay out the sheet of plastic on the table and secure the edges with sticky tape. This prevents the sheet from sliding around and disrupting your experiment.

3 Hold the fork with your ungloved hand. As you bring the fork close to the dish, you should see a spark jump. It is easier to see this in the dark.

2 Put the rubber glove on one hand. Slide the metal dish back and forth over the plastic sheet for a few minutes. This will charge the dish with static electricity.

FLOOD AND DROUGHT

Playtime
The flooded streets of Pahang, Malaysia, are a playground for some, but most people are mopping up the water after it has swept through their houses.

FLOODING (too much water) and drought (too little water) can have a devastating effect on the environment and the people who live in it. The people who live in these areas have to try to deal with these extreme conditions.

In some parts of the world, flooding occurs regularly in certain seasons, such as during the summer monsoons in India. Sometimes, flooding can be caused by cyclones. In February 2000, a cyclone with winds blowing at up to 260km/h caused widespread flooding in Mozambique. Tens of thousands of people were killed or made homeless as vast areas of land became submerged in water. Sudden flooding following heavy rains can be equally destructive. In December 1999, prolonged rain created terrible mudslides that buried or swept away whole towns and villages along the northern coast of Venezuela.

At the same time, east Africa was suffering from severe drought. Two years had passed without the usual seasonal rains. The crops had failed, livestock were dying in their thousands and much of the population were suffering from malnutrition.

A dangerous delta
A Bangladeshi family stands by the remains of their home after a devastating storm in the Ganges Delta. A cyclone has surged inland from the Indian Ocean, crossed the flat Delta region, and flattened everything in its path.

Breaking records
A weather satellite image reveals the extent of the flooding of the Missouri and Mississippi rivers in the USA in July 1993. The city of St Louis is coloured purple at the bottom of the picture. In the summer of 1993, the American Midwest suffered the worst flooding since records began. River levels rose up to 15m above normal.

Around the waterhole

Animals gather around a waterhole during the dry season on the east African savanna. During the dry season no rain falls at all. All the water dries up, and the vegetation available for the animals to graze on gets scarcer. Only a few waterholes are left, but even these will shrink as the Sun relentlessly beats down on the plains.

Death in the drought

In 1992, parts of east Africa suffered one of the worst droughts ever recorded. Crops were devastated, and livestock such as cattle were killed by the thousand.

Dry and lifeless

These trees have died through lack of water. Drought is caused by a lack of precipitation, but it can also be caused by hot, dry winds and frequent fires. These elements combine to take moisture from the soil and use up groundwater beneath the top levels of the soil.

Aid for Ethiopia

Families from Ethiopia in east Africa gather at an aid centre to collect food. Ethiopia is one of the world's poorest countries. Most people live by farming the land, but drought results in a very poor harvest and widespread famine. In 1984, more than 800,000 people are known to have died in one of the worst droughts seen to date.

GAUGING THE RAIN

THE amount of precipitation (rain, sleet, snow or dew) that falls from the atmosphere varies widely throughout the world. Heavy rain falls regularly in tropical regions around the Equator. Here, the air contains plenty of moisture evaporated from the warm oceans. The summer monsoon rains that occur over southern Asia can reach record amounts. Cherrapunji in north-eastern India receives an average of 10m of rainfall each year, most of which falls during the summer monsoon between April and October. These rains are essential to the agriculture of southern Asia. Since so many people depend on the monsoon to survive, meteorologists need to predict how much rain will fall so that food crops will grow.

How much rainfall do you get where you live? Make this simple rain gauge to measure the amount. Meteorologists use a similar rain gauge at many weather stations around the world. If it is very rainy where you live, this project will keep you busy, but if you live in a desert region, you may have to wait a long time for any rain!

Keeping dry
Umbrellas were probably invented in China as early as the 2nd century BC.

MEASURING RAINFALL

You will need: scissors, sticky tape, large jar (such as a sweet jar), ruler, ballpoint pen, large plastic funnel, tall narrow jar or bottle, notebook.

1 Cut a piece of tape to the height of the jar and stick it on. Mark a scale on the tape at 1cm intervals. Measure the diameter of the jar and cut the funnel to the same size.

2 Place the funnel in the jar. Put the gauge outside in an open space away from any trees. Look at the gauge at the same time each day. Has it rained in the last 24 hours?

3 If it has rained, use the scale to se how much water is in the jar. Th is the rainfall for the past 24 hours. Make a note of the reading. Empty the jar before you return it to its place

Being more precise

Measure rainfall more accurately by using a separate narrow measuring jar. Cut a length of tape to the height of the narrow jar and stick it to the side. Pour some water into the large collecting jar up to the 1cm mark. Now pour this water into the smaller measuring bottle. Mark 1cm where the water level reaches. Divide the length from the bottom of the bottle to the 1cm mark into 10 equal parts. Each mark you make will be equivalent to 1mm of rainfall. Extend the scale past the 1cm mark to the top of the measuring bottle.

All-in-one weather instrument

You can buy an all-in-one weather instrument, which measures temperature, rainfall, wind direction and wind speed. These are handy if you don't have much space to set up lots of equipment.

Automatic weather station

Meteorologists use all-in-one weather instruments to measure different features of the weather. These instruments automatically monitor local weather conditions, such as wind speed and direction, air pressure, temperature, humidity and solar radiation.

FACT BOX

• The wettest place in the world is Mawsynram in India. Here, an average of nearly 12m of rain falls every year.

• New York and Sydney have a little over 1m of rain a year. Paris and London have about 60cm a year.

• The driest place in the world is the Atacama Desert, west of the Andes in Chile, South America. In parts of the desert just a few showers fall every 100 years.

• Sea storms can cause worse flooding than rainfall. The large waves that form can submerge coastal areas.

SNOW AND ICE

SNOW falls in winter in many countries. It also falls all year round in places near the North and South poles and at the top of mountains. Most of the precipitation that actually reaches the ground starts as snow. At the top of high clouds the temperature is below the freezing point of water, and ice crystals form. Ice crystals join together to form snowflakes that fall from the clouds when the snowflakes become too heavy. If the lower air is warm, however, the snowflakes will melt and turn into rain. A mixture of snow and rain sometimes falls as sleet. This occurs when the falling snowflakes start to melt and then turn back into ice as they pass through a freezing layer of air.

On many winter nights the ground becomes snow-white even when it has not been snowing. This white covering is called frost, which forms when the ground gets cold and water vapour in the air condenses on it. The water immediately freezes into tiny sparkling crystals of ice.

Works of art
Snowflakes are made up of masses of tiny ice crystals. Under a microscope, the most common snowflake form is a branching star shape called a dendrite.

Death in the valley
In February 1999, an avalanche devastated a village in the Chamonix Valley in the French Alps. About 40,000 tonnes of snow hurtled down the mountain slopes at 200km/h. The snow buried houses and cars, killing 12 people.

Avalanche!
Thousands of tonnes of snow break loose in an avalanche on Mount Everest in the Himalayas. Avalanches career downhill at tremendous speeds, destroying everything in their path. They occur when the weight of the snow on the mountain exceeds the forces of gravity and friction that hold the snow in place.

Ice on glass

Ice crystals have formed on a windowpane. If glass gets very cold, water vapour in the air condenses on it, forming crystals where it freezes.

Jack Frost

Jack Frost is a mythical character who is thought to make the beautiful icy patterns you find outside on trees, plants and fences during cold weather.

Chunks of ice

Most of the ice in the world is found in the ice caps in the Arctic and Antarctic. Around 6 million sq km of ice cover the Arctic Ocean in the north. This huge ice pack is broken into large floes (sea ice) by the wind and ocean currents. Antarctica is covered by a permanent ice cap, which is over 3km thick at the centre of the continent.

Ice storms in Quebec

During the winter of 1998, the province of Quebec in Canada suffered a storm of icy rain that lasted for a whole week. Ice up to 8cm thick collected on trees, electricity pylons and cables. The ice was so heavy that trees and pylons collapsed, resulting in widespread damage and disruption. The more remote areas of Quebec did not have any electricity for a month. Many farmers lost livestock because they could no longer feed them or keep them warm. This was the worst ice storm experienced in this region for at least 100 years.

COPING WITH COLD

ONLY a tiny proportion of animals and plants live in the cold temperate regions in the far north of North America, Europe and Asia and in the polar regions around the North and South poles. In these areas the winters are long, and temperatures often fall below −50°C. The plants and animals that live in these bitterly cold parts of the world are well adapted to the environment. The main plants are evergreen conifer trees. These form a great northern, or boreal, forest region that spans the continents of North America, Europe and Asia.

The largest animals of the boreal forests are caribou and moose (elk). These animals have thick fur and can survive on almost any type of vegetation. They shelter in the forests in the winter but venture on to open ground farther north in summer. This open ground is called the tundra, which is covered by snow and ice for most of the year. A few metres below the surface, the ground is permanently frozen. It is too cold for trees to grow, so grasses and low shrubs make up the vegetation. These plants make the most of the short summer months by growing, flowering and seeding rapidly.

Farther north still, on the permanently frozen north polar ice cap, plants do not grow. Polar bears hunt seals that swim in the icy waters of the Arctic Ocean. Polar bears have thick fur with a layer of fat underneath to protect their bodies against the cold. Seals and whales have a thick layer of blubber beneath the skin to insulate them from the cold. Seals and whales are also found around Antarctica at the opposite end of the Earth.

Needle leaves
The needle-like leaves of these conifers in the Rocky Mountains of North America lose much less heat than broad leaves would.

Blubber is best
Seals spend a lot of time swimming in the ice-cold waters of the Arctic and Antarctic oceans. Seals are warm-blooded, which means they can regulate their own body heat. Under their skin, a fat-filled layer of spongy tissue, called blubber, insulates their bodies from the cold.

Penguin playground
Adelie penguins gather on the ice along the coast of Antarctica. The temperatures can drop to as low as −90°C in Antarctica. Penguins are protected from the severe cold by their closely packed, oily feathers and an insulating layer of fat under their skin.

Saami in the snow

A caribou herder from Kataukeino in northern Norway relaxes on his snow scooter during the spring migration of caribou. He is one of the Saami people from northern Scandinavia, and is dressed in traditional clothing – a parka and trousers made out of animal skins and trimmed with fur. These warm clothes will insulate him against the bitter cold of the Scandinavian tundra.

Fruit of the tundra

Arctic plants flower when the ground is barely free of snow, taking advantage of the short summer. The ground over the permanently frozen layer of soil, called permafrost, thaws in the summer. The plants then get a roothold. They cannot develop deep roots because of the solid layer of permafrost.

Like father, like son

An Inuit father and his son live in the Northwest Territories of Canada, which has one of the coldest climates on the Earth. Their bodies are well adapted to the climate. They are short, stocky and their faces have grown used to the cold. Inuit people have a very fatty diet to build up a thick layer of fat.

The treeless tundra

It is summer and the lower slopes of the mountains in Denali National Park, Alaska, USA, have lost their covering of snow. Although the ground just below the surface is still frozen, plants such as grasses and low shrubs can still survive.

ICE AGE OR GREENHOUSE?

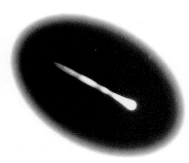

Ball of fire

A shooting star, or meteor, streaks through the atmosphere. Shooting stars are streaks of light created when lumps of rock and dust hurtle towards the Earth and burn up in the Earth's atmosphere. Parts of a rock often fall to the ground as meteorites. If a large meteorite hits the Earth enough material can be thrown into the atmosphere to bring about a change in climate. This may have caused the extinction of the dinosaurs some 65 million years ago.

Throughout the history of the Earth, the climate has undergone many changes. Over the past million years or so, the climate has alternated between periods of warmth and cold. During the cold periods, called ice ages, most of North America and Europe became covered in vast sheets of ice. The last cold period lasted until about 25,000 years ago. Scientists used to think that another ice age was approaching. In fact, the atmosphere has been warming at a dramatic rate since the 1970s. This may be due to a number of reasons.

Most importantly, humans are burning more and more fuels, such as coal and oil, which creates carbon dioxide. This gas is building up in the atmosphere, trapping the Sun's heat. As a result, the atmosphere acts rather like a greenhouse. As more and more carbon dioxide builds up in the atmosphere, this so-called "greenhouse effect" warms the climate. Scientists think that if humans continue to produce carbon dioxide by burning fossil fuels, the Earth's climate will warm by several degrees in the next 50 years. This may make the polar ice caps melt, causing sea levels to rise and flooding many countries. Rising temperatures also alter wind patterns and ocean currents, disrupting weather patterns and climates throughout the world.

Holding back the tides

The Thames Flood Barrier at Woolwich in London will prevent the city from being flooded in case of an exceptionally high tide. If the greenhouse effect becomes a reality, this preventative measure may save millions of people who live in the city.

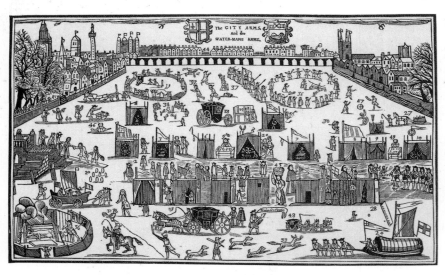

Frozen over

A change in the heat output of the Sun may have caused the Little Ice Age that occurred in the 1600s. During this time, the River Thames in London froze so hard that a series of frost fairs could be held on it. The picture above shows the Frost Fair that was held in 1683.

The ash clouds of Pinatubo

After lying dormant (sleeping) for more than 500 years, the volcano Mount Pinatubo erupted in June 1991. As the volcano erupted, it threw vast clouds of ash high into the air, blocking light from the Sun for days. Torrential rains followed the eruption and caused mud and ash slides, which devastated the surrounding countryside. Ash particles in the atmosphere were also responsible for cooler summers around the world for several years.

Ozone hole

In the 1980s, scientists discovered that the ozone layer, part of the Earth's atmosphere, was thinning over Antarctica. If the ozone layer becomes too thin, it will let more rays through from the Sun, which will harm the Earth.

Cycle safely

A cyclist wears a protective face mask to filter out the harmful fumes of busy city traffic. Gases released by car engines are now known to be responsible, in part, for the greenhouse effect.

SOHO image

The SOlar Heliospheric Observatory (SOHO) space probe took this picture of the scorching surface of the Sun. Using space observatories such as these, meteorologists learn more about how and why changes take place in the Sun's energy output.

STUDYING THE WEATHER

METEOROLOGISTS do two main jobs. They collect data and process information about the weather from day to day. Then they use this information to help them forecast future weather trends. Meteorologists collect information from weather stations scattered all over the world. They use a variety of measuring instruments. Thermometers measure the temperature, barometers measure air pressure and hygrometers measure the humidity of the air. Weather vanes show the direction of the wind and anemometers measure its speed.

Increasingly meteorologists are turning to space technology to help them. They send weather satellites into orbit to take pictures of clouds and measure weather conditions in the air. Satellites are useful because they can record weather in remote regions where there are no weather stations.

Blast-off
A rocket blasts off from Cape Canaverel, Florida, in the USA. The rocket is carrying a weather satellite that will orbit the Earth and send images to meteorologists back on Earth, along with other weather data.

Cloud in the north
A number of satellite pictures have been joined together to give a true colour image of the Earth. The polar ice cap at the North Pole is shown at the top here. Thick cloud covers the pole and reaches into the North Atlantic Ocean.

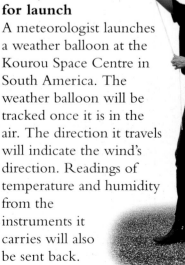

Ready for launch
A meteorologist launches a weather balloon at the Kourou Space Centre in South America. The weather balloon will be tracked once it is in the air. The direction it travels will indicate the wind's direction. Readings of temperature and humidity from the instruments it carries will also be sent back.

Measuring sunshine

A sunshine recorder is made up of a glass ball that acts rather like a lens. When the Sun shines, the glass ball focuses the light on to a sheet of paper below the ball. The focused light leaves a scorch mark on the paper that is matched to a calibrated time scale. In this way, the meteorologist can record how long the Sun shines each day.

Weather at sea

An automatic weather buoy carries many types of weather-recording devices, such as anemometers, barometers, hygrometers and thermometers. The readings from the different instruments are transmitted by radio to weather stations or passing satellites.

Head for the clouds

A pilot flies his plane straight into a storm. He works for the National Weather Service in the USA. The plane is a specially strengthened aircraft that can cope with violent air currents, lightning and bombardment by hailstones. Instruments beneath the wings monitor weather conditions.

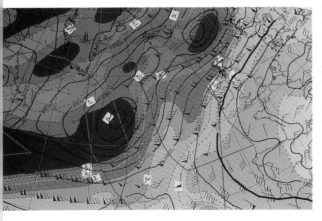

Storm map

A computer map is used to predict the likelihood of a storm in the Atlantic Ocean. The solid lines are called isobars and link regions of equal air pressure. Storms often occur in regions where the isobars are close together.

Computer forecasting

Meteorologists use computers to predict how the weather will change. This can help them make more accurate forecasts.

YOUR WEATHER STATION

How hot is it?
A thermometer must always be kept in the shade to measure the air temperature accurately. If the device is left in direct sunlight, the liquid will also absorb energy from the Sun. As a result, the thermometer will indicate a temperature higher than the actual air temperature.

METEOROLOGISTS work at about 12,000 weather stations worldwide, gathering information about the weather. They feed the data they gather from satellites, balloons, weather buoys and other instruments into powerful computers to provide them with an overall view of the weather and how it may change. Using this information, they can draw weather maps that show the state of the weather at any one time, using symbols to represent conditions such as rainfall, wind direction and pressure. They also use this information to draw other charts that they use to make a forecast of the weather.

You can set up your own weather station to record weather conditions with a few simple instruments. You will be able to use some of the instruments you have made in earlier projects, such as the weather vane, hygrometer and rain gauge. In addition, you will need to buy a thermometer and a barometer (which measures air pressure), both of which can be bought fairly cheaply.

Pine station
No home weather station would be complete without pine cones. When they are ripe, pine cones open on dry days to release their seeds. They close up if the weather is humid or damp.

Make a note
Take measurements with your weather instruments every day. Write them down in a special weather book. Also, make a note of what the weather is like generally – fine, cloudy, drizzle, frosty and so on. Don't forget to make a note of the date!

How much did it rain?
Your rain gauge will tell you this. Measure the amount of water in the jar. Use the measuring bottle to be more accurate. Always empty the jar when you have finished.

Dry or damp

Seaweed is a useful item to have in your weather station. Like pine cones, seaweed changes as the humidity changes. If the weather is dry, the seaweed feels dry and brittle. If the weather is humid, however, the seaweed feels flexible and damp.

Cumulus clouds

As well as using the instruments you have made to predict what the weather will be like, you can make general predictions, too. Studying the clouds is often a good way of telling what sort of weather is in store. Puffy cumulus clouds that grow in size and turn darker suggest that there could soon be showers. However, these clouds are scattered, so showers will not last for long.

Red skies

Red clouds at dawn is often a sign that rain is on the way. A red sky at night, however, can be a good sign, promising that the next day will be fine. An old saying sums this up with the words "Red sky at night, shepherd's delight. Red sky in the morning, shepherd's warning."

How humid is it?

Your hygrometer will help. Note the position of the pointer on the scale. When the pointer tilts up, the air is moist and rain could be on the way.

Which way is the wind blowing?

Remember that the arrow on your weather vane points in the direction from which the wind is blowing. So a north wind blows from the north.

GLOSSARY

A

active volcano
A volcano that is erupting or might erupt at any time in the near future.

anemometer
An instrument used in weather forecasting to measure the speed and force of the wind.

archipelago
A large group of islands.

atmosphere
The layer of air surrounding the Earth.

atmospheric pressure
A measure of the weight of the atmosphere pressing down on the surface of the Earth.

atoll
A small island made up of an almost circular strip of coral surrounding a lagoon of sea water.

B

barometer
An instrument used in weather forecasting to measure the pressure of the atmosphere.

Beaufort scale
A range of code numbers that is used to describe the force of the wind, from 0 (calm) to 12 (hurricane force). The Beaufort scale is named after British naval officer Sir Francis Beaufort, who formulated it.

C

Celsius scale
A scale for measuring temperature where 0 degrees is assigned to the temperature at which water freezes and 100 degrees to the temperature at which water boils. The scale was introduced by Swedish astronomer Anders Celsius.

climate
The typical weather pattern of a place during the year.

condensation
The process by which water vapour becomes a liquid.

constructive boundary
The edge of one of the Earth's plates, where new plate material is forming.

continental drift
The gradual movement of the continents across the face of the Earth.

core
The region at the centre of the Earth.

Coriolis force
A theoretical force that results from the Earth's rotation in space. The Coriolis force causes moving particles, including the wind, to deflect to the right in the Northern Hemisphere and to the left in the Southern Hemisphere.

creepmeter
An instrument that measures movements of the Earth's crust along faults in the crust.

crust
The rocky surface layer of the Earth.

cyclone
An area of low pressure into which winds spiral clockwise in the Southern Hemisphere and counter-clockwise in the Northern Hemisphere. This weather condition is usually associated with a violent tropical storm.

D

destructive boundary
A region of the Earth's crust where one of the plates of the crust is colliding with another and being destroyed.

dew
Water that condenses on to objects near the ground when they are much cooler than the surrounding air.

doldrums
The region near the Equator that is characterized by low pressure and light, shifting winds.

dormant volcano
A volcano that is not active at present but might erupt one day in the future. The word dormant means sleeping.

drought
A long time without rain, when living things do not have the water they need.

dust devil
A small, rapidly rotating wind that is visible due to the dust it picks up from the ground as it rotates.

E

earthquake
An often violent shaking of the Earth's crust, caused when plates in the crust try to slide past or over each other.

El Niño
A major ocean-warming event that begins along the coast of Peru and triggers weather extremes, which happen once every three to seven years.

epicentre
The region on the Earth's surface that lies directly above the focus of an earthquake.

Equator
The imaginary circle around the middle of the Earth between the North and South poles. This region has a climate that stays hot all year round because it always gets the greatest amount of direct sunlight as the Earth turns on its axis.

erosion
The gradual wearing away of the Earth's surface by the action of wind, rain, heat, cold, and the movement of rivers.

exosphere
The outermost layer of the Earth's atmosphere that forms a boundary with space.

extensometer
An instrument that measures whether stretching movements are occurring in the rocks in the Earth's crust.

extinct volcano
A volcano that has not erupted for many years and is believed unlikely ever to erupt again.

F

Fahrenheit scale
A scale for measuring temperature at which 32 degrees is assigned to the temperature at which water freezes and 212 degrees to the temperature at which water boils. The scale was formulated by Gabriel Daniel Fahrenheit.

fault
A crack in the Earth's crust.

focus
The exact point underground where the rocks in the Earth's crust move and cause an earthquake.

fossil
The remains in the Earth's rocks of living things that have died and been preserved.

front
The point or boundary where two air masses that have different temperatures and different amounts of moisture meet. When two fronts meet, there is a change in the weather.

fumarole
An opening in the ground in volcanic regions, where steam and gases escape.

G

geologist
A scientist who carries out the study of the Earth's surface and rocks.

geology
The scientific study of the Earth and the changes that take place on its surface and in the rocks below.

geothermal energy
The energy created in areas of volcanic activity by the heating of rocks below the Earth's surface.

geyser
A fountain of steam and water that spurts out of vents in the ground in volcanic regions.

gravimeter
An instrument that measures slight changes in gravity in the rocks in the Earth's crust.

greenhouse effect
The way certain gases in the Earth's atmosphere trap the Sun's heat like the panes of glass in a greenhouse. The effect increases the temperature of the Earth's surface and lower atmosphere.

Gulf Stream
A warm, swift, narrow ocean current flowing along the east coast of the USA and towards western Europe.

H

halo
Rings that encircle the Sun or Moon when seen through a cloud composed of ice crystals or a sky filled with ice crystals. The effect is due to the refraction of light.

hot spot
A place in the Earth's crust away from plate boundaries where hot rock forces its way to the surface to cause volcanoes.

hot springs
Places in volcanic regions where water that has been heated underground by rocks bubbles to the surface.

humidity
A measure of the amount of water, or moisture, in the air.

hurricane
A severe tropical cyclone with wind speeds of over 125km/h.

hygrometer
An instrument used in weather forecasting to measure humidity.

I
igneous rock
A rock that forms when magma (hot molten rock) cools and becomes solid. This can happen both on the Earth's surface or underground.

intrusive rock
A rock that forms underground when hot molten rock forces its way into existing rock layers and then cools.

L
land breeze
A gentle wind that blows from the land towards the sea.

La Niña
An event in which the central and eastern tropical Pacific Ocean turns cooler than normal.

lava
The molten rock that pours out of volcanoes on to the surface of the ground and then cools. Lava can be very thin and runny or thick and pasty.

M
magma
The name given to hot molten rock while it is still inside the Earth's crust.

mantle
The very deep layer of rock that lies underneath the Earth's crust.

mesosphere
The layer of Earth's atmosphere between the stratosphere and the thermosphere.

metamorphic rock
Rock that forms when existing rocks are changed because of great heat and pressure inside the Earth's crust.

meteorologist
A person who studies the science of meteorology (weather study) and forecasts and reports on the weather.

meteorology
A science that studies the atmosphere, climates and weather conditions in regions throughout the world.

mineral
A chemical compound found inside the Earth.

monsoon
A wind that reverses its direction in winter and summer. Monsoon winds commonly affect southern Asia around the Indian Ocean, often bringing heavy rains in the summer season.

N
nuée ardente
A glowing cloud of very hot air and ash given out by some volcanoes. It spreads quickly over the area surrounding the volcano, causing death and destruction on a large scale.

O
ozone
A form of oxygen that exists in a layer of the Earth's atmosphere that blocks dangerous rays from the Sun.

P
P waves
The primary waves produced by an earthquake that travel fastest and are detected first.

planet
One of the nine large bodies in the Solar System that circle around the Sun. The Earth is one of the nine planets.

plate
A section of the Earth's crust that moves in a recognized direction across the Earth's surface.

precipitation
Any form of water that comes out of the air and falls to the ground.

prevailing winds
The wind direction most frequently observed during a given period.

R
radiosonde
A scientific instrument carried high into the air, usually by a weather balloon. The radiosonde sends information back to Earth about the atmosphere and weather conditions.

Richter scale
A scale for measuring the strength of earthquakes, devised by the American scientist Charles Richter.

S
S waves
The secondary waves produced by an earthquake, detected later than P waves.

satellite
A spacecraft that circles around the Earth in orbit. It sends information back to scientists on Earth to help them study the world's climates and weather.

savanna
A huge region of grassland typically found in a tropical climate.

sea breeze
A gentle wind that blows from the sea towards the land.

sedimentary rock
Rock formed from layers of sediments, or materials such as eroded rock and chemical compounds that settled in layers millions of years ago at the bottom of seas and rivers.

seismogram
The wavy trace on paper that a seismograph makes.

seismograph
An instrument used by scientists to record earthquake waves.

seismologist
A geologist who carries out the study of earthquake waves.

seismology
The study of the waves that earthquakes send out.

Solar System
The family of planets, moons and other bodies that orbit round the Sun.

spectrum
The spread of colours found in white light in the order red, orange, yellow, green, blue, indigo and violet. A spectrum appears when white light passes through a prism (a transparent solid object such as a wedge of glass) or through raindrops to form a rainbow.

stratosphere
An upper layer of the Earth's atmosphere, above the clouds.

T

thermocouple
A thermometer scientists use to measure very high temperatures.

thermometer
An instrument that is used for measuring temperature.

thermosphere
A layer of the Earth's atmosphere above the mesosphere, beginning about 80km above the Earth's surface.

tidal wave
A huge ocean wave caused when an earthquake takes place on the seabed. It has nothing to do with tides.

tiltmeter
An instrument used to detect the tilting of the ground.

tornado
An intense, rapidly rotating column of air that extends from a thundercloud in the shape of a funnel.

transpiration
The process in the water cycle by which plants release water vapour into the air. The vapour will eventually turn back into liquid and fall back to the Earth as some form of precipitation.

tremor
A shaking of the ground.

trench
A valley in the seabed, marking the region where one plate of the Earth's crust meets another and is forced down into the crust.

tropics
Part of the Earth's surface that lies between the Tropic of Cancer (at a latitude of 23.5 degrees north of the Equator) and the Tropic of Capricorn (at a latitude of 23.5 degrees south of the Equator).

troposphere
The layer of the Earth's atmosphere closest to the surface of the Earth, where clouds form.

tsunami
A huge ocean wave set up when an earthquake takes place on the seabed. It is popularly called a tidal wave.

tundra
A huge treeless area in the Arctic region that has very long, harsh winters and where the ground beneath the surface is always frozen, even in the summer.

typhoon
A hurricane that forms over the western Pacific Ocean.

V

vent
An opening in the ground.

viscosity
A measure of how thick or thin a liquid is. A liquid with low viscosity flows faster than one with a high viscosity.

volcanic bomb
A lump of molten material flung into the air from a volcano.

volcano
An opening in the Earth's crust from which molten rock escapes.

W

waterspout
A column of rotating wind over water that has characteristics of a dust devil and a tornado.

weather
The condition of the atmosphere at any particular time and place.

wind
Air moving in relation to the Earth's surface.

INDEX

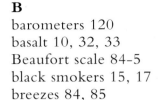

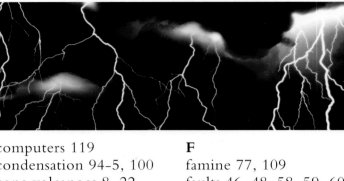

A

aa lava 22, 24
active volcanoes 22
air 80-4
air pressure 84-5, 119
Alaska 47, 50, 51
altitude 73, 74, 81
Anchorage 47
andesite 32, 33, 34
anemometers 90
animals 72-3, 75, 79,
    109, 114
Antarctica 55, 59
ash clouds 8, 22, 23,
    26, 27, 30, 36, 37, 42,
    43, 62
atmosphere 42, 43 68,
    80-2
atmospheric pressure 84
atolls 21, 23
aurora australis 80
aurora borealis 80
avalanches 112

B

barometers 120
basalt 10, 32, 33
Beaufort scale 84-5
black smokers 15, 17
breezes 84, 85

C

cacti 79
caldera 23
Canary Islands 21, 27, 32
carbon dioxide 12, 13,
    26, 27, 28, 29, 38,
    82, 116
Caribbean 26, 27, 46, 62
Chichon El, 42
China 47, 55, 59
cirrus clouds 98-9
climate 42-3, 72-3, 74,
    76, 78, 101
climate changes 116
climatic zones 72-3
clouds 68, 92-3, 94-5,
    98-100, 112
cold, adaptation
    to 114-15
cold temperate climates
    72-3

computers 119
condensation 94-5, 100
cone volcanoes 8, 22
constructive boundary 14
continents 14, 18
coral islands 21
core, Earth's 11
Coriolis effect 84
craters 21, 23, 30, 42, 45
creepmeters 58, 60
crust 4, 10, 11, 14, 46, 48
crystals 32, 34
cumulus clouds 98-9,
    100, 121
currents, rock 16
cyclones 92-3, 108

D

dehydration 78
deserts 67, 72, 73, 78-9,
    111
destructive boundary 18
dew 100
droughts 76-7, 108-9
dust devils 88
dykes 32

E

earthquakes 4, 8, 9, 10,
    46-63
El Niño 76-7
electricity 104-7
electromagnetic radiation
    68
energy, geothermal 39
epicentre, earthquakes
    50, 56
Equator 68, 72
eruptions 12-3, 22-3, 26,
    28, 30-1, 34, 36, 42-3
Etna, Mount 29, 37, 58
evaporation 94-5
explosive volcanoes 22,
    23, 26, 28, 30-1, 32,
    34, 42
extensometers 60

F

famine 77, 109
faults 46, 48, 58, 59, 60
fissure volcanoes 23, 43
floods 67, 76-7, 92, 108,
    111, 116
focus, earthquakes 50
fog 95
forest fires 77
fossils 42
frost 112-13
Fuji, Mount 23
fumaroles 27, 38, 40

G

Galapagos Islands 15
gases 12, 22, 23, 26, 27,
    28-9, 34, 58, 82-3, 116
geothermal energy 39
geothermal features 9,
    38-9
geysers 38, 39, 40
Giant's Causeway 10
global warming 76, 116
Grand Canyon 11
granite 34
gravimeters 60
greenhouse effect 116
groundwater 94
Gulf Stream 74

H

hailstones 104
Hawaii 9, 12, 20-1, 22,
    23, 24, 32, 47, 58
Hawaiian volcanoes 23
heat, adaptation to 78-9
helium 82
Herculaneum 26
Himalayas 19
hot spots 20-1, 22, 32
hot springs 9, 38, 39, 40
humidity 96-7
hurricanes 92-3
hygrometers 96-7,
    120

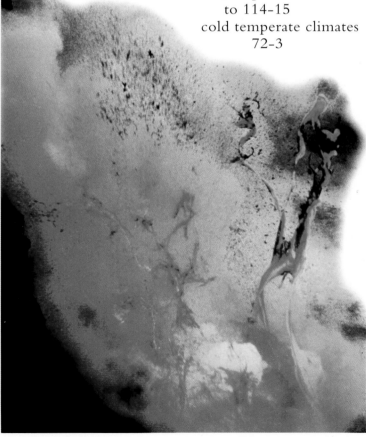

I

ice ages 116
ice caps 113, 114, 116
ice storms 113
Iceland 11, 15, 36, 38, 39, 43
igneous rocks 32, 35
Indonesia, 8, 19, 22, 27, 37, 43
intrusions 32, 34, 35
Io 44, 45
islands 20-1
isobars 119

J

Japan 8, 23, 47, 50, 59, 62, 63
Jupiter 44, 45

K

Kilauea 9, 20, 21, 22, 23, 32, 58
Kobe 8, 47, 49, 50, 53, 59, 62, 63
Krakatoa 8, 42, 51

L

La Niña 76-7
landscapes 36-7
Lanzarote 21, 32
lava 4, 8, 10, 12, 22, 23, 24-5, 26, 32-3, 34, 58
light 102-3
lightning 104-7

M

mackerel sky 98
magma 8, 10, 14, 16, 20, 22, 23, 31, 34, 38, 40
mantle 10, 11, 16, 18, 20
Mars 9, 44
Mauna Loa 12, 20, 22
measurement 118-21
   humidity 96-7
   rainfall 110-11
   temperature 70-1
   wind 90-1
Mercalli, Giuseppe 54
metamorphic rocks 34
meteorites 11
meteorologists 66, 111, 118-21
meteors and meteorites 116

mid-ocean ridges 14-15, 18, 32
minerals 14, 15, 38, 39
monsoons 101, 108, 110
Moon 9, 44, 45, 55
Mount St Helens 30-1, 36, 42
mountains 73, 81, 95, 112
mudslides 93, 108, 117

N

New Guinea 43
New Zealand 19, 38, 40
nimbus clouds 98-9, 100
nitrogen 82
Northern Hemisphere 69, 84
northern lights 80
nuée ardente 26

O

obsidian, 33
ocean currents 74, 76, 116
oceans 14, 18, 19, 74, 76, 94-5
oxygen 26, 28, 29, 82
ozone 80, 95
ozone layer 80, 117

P

P waves 52, 54
Pacific Ocean 14, 18, 19, 20, 21, 22, 76
pahoehoe lava 22, 24, 33
Palmieri, Luigi 56
pasty lava 23, 24, 34
Pele 20, 21, 23
Pelean volcanoes 23
Pinatubo, Mount 42, 43
pine cones 120
planets 9, 44-5
plants 72, 94, 96-7, 109, 114-15
plastic flow 16
plates 14, 15, 18-9, 20, 46
Plinian volcanoes 23
pollution 80, 81, 95, 117
Pompeii 26, 27, 28
precipitation 77, 94-5, 100-01, 110-12
pumice 33, 34

Q

quiet volcanoes 22, 26

R

rain 94-5, 100-1, 110-11
rain gauges 110-11, 120
rainbows 102-3
rainforests 72, 96
recording measurements 120
Richter scale 54
Ring of Fire 19, 22
rocks 10, 11, 16, 24, 32-3, 34, 36, 50
ropy lava 33

S

S waves 52
San Andreas fault 46, 48, 51, 60
San Francisco 46, 47, 50
satellites 59
savannas 72-3
sea mounts 20
sea-floor spreading 14-15
seasons 69, 74
seaweed 121
sedimentary rocks 11, 32
seismic waves 54
seismograms 54
seismographs 54, 55, 56-7, 60
seismologists 54-5, 56, 59, 60
shield volcanoes 22, 24, 45
sleet 112
smog 95
snow 66, 112
soil 10, 36, 37
solar power 69
Solar System 9, 44-5
Southern Hemisphere 69, 84
southern lights 80
static electricity 106-7
Stevenson screen 71
storms
   thunder 88, 100, 104
   tropical 67, 92-3
stratosphere 80
stratus clouds 98-9
Strombolian volcanoes 23
submarine volcanoes 23

sulphur 15, 38, 42, 43, 44, 45
Sun
   heat source 68, 94, 116, 117
   protection from 66, 74, 78-9
Sunset Crater 27
sunsets 81
sunshine, measurement 119
Surtsey 15

T

tarpit 38
Teide, Mount 21, 23, 27
temperatures 16, 24, 38, 40, 43, 58
   changes 74-5, 116-17
   measurement 70-1
thermocouples 58
thermometers 58, 70-1, 96, 120
thunderstorms 88, 100, 104
tidal waves 8, 50, 51, 92-3
tiltmeters 60, 61
tornadoes 67, 88-9
trade winds 76, 84
transpiration 94, 97
tremors 48, 54, 55
trenches 18, 19
Triton 44
tropical climates 72

tropical storms 67, 92-3
tsunamis 50, 51
tundra 72, 73, 114-15
Turkey 51, 63
twisters 67, 88-9
typhoons 92-3

U
umbrellas 110

V
vents 15, 23, 27
Venus 9, 44, 45
Vesuvius, Mount 26, 27, 37, 55, 58
viscosity 24
volcanic bombs 23, 27
volcanoes 4, 117
volcanologists 8, 9, 27, 58, 59
volcanology 8
Vulcanian volcanoes 23

W
warm temperate climates 72-3
water 10, 12, 38-9, 40
water cycle 94-5

water vapour 94-5, 96-7, 98, 100-1, 112-13
waterspouts 88-9
waves, earthquakes 52-3, 54
weather 5, 22, 42-3
weather balloons 118
weather buoys 119
weather forecasts 118-21
weather maps 120
weather satellites 118
weather stations 111, 120-21
weather vanes 90-1, 120
whirlwinds 88-9
wind 84-5, 88-93, 109
wind belts 84, 116
wind power 85
wind-chill 70

Y
Yellowstone National Park 5, 9, 39

Z
Zaire 37

ACKNOWLEDGEMENTS

The publishers would like to thank the following children for modelling in this book: Maria Bloodworth, Tony Borg, Steven Briggs, Anum Butt, Dima Degtyarov, Roxanne Game, Fawwaz Ghany, Angelica Hambrier, Larrissa Henderson, Lori Hey, Jackie Ishiekwene, Daniel Johnson, Jon Leaning, Louis Loucaides, Erin Macarthy, Hanife Manur, Tanya Martin, Malak Mroue, Lola Olayinka, Tom Swaine-Jameson, Ini Usoro and Sophie Viner. Additional thanks to Caroline Beattie and to West Meters Ltd for the loan of props.

PICTURE CREDITS b=bottom, t=top, c=centre, l=left, r=right
Bryan & Cherry Alexander: 50bl. Ardea/R Gibbons: 23tl; /F Gohier: 21b; /A Warren: 39cl. The Art Archive: 68tl. BBC Natural History Unit/B Davidson: 37br; /C Buxton: 36bl; /Doug Wechsler: 77cl. Biofotos: 31tr; /B Rogers: 36br; /S Summerhays: 12tr, 58br. Bridgeman Art Library: CEPHAS/M Rock: 37bl. Bruce Coleman: 72bl, 114cl, 11br; /C Atlantide: 26br; /F Bruemmer: 37c; /G Cubitt: 19cr; /M Freeman: 62t, 105br; /Tore Hagman: 99cl; /Johnny Johnson: 115tr; /Dr Scott Nielsen: 98br, 99tl & 99br; /Mary Plage: 101br; /John Shaw: 75bl; /Kim Taylor: 100cr. Mary Evans Picture Library: 104tl, 116bl; /A Rackham: 113tr. FLPA/M Withers: 31bl; /S Ardito(Panda Photo): 55tr; /S Jonasson: 15cr; /S McCutcheon: 51cl. Gamma/Frank Spooner: 27cl, 49br, 51t, 62br, 62bl, 63cl, 63br, 63bl. Genesis Space Photo Library: 55tl. Geoscience Features Library: 94tl. Hulton Getty: 84cr & 90c. Getty One Stone: 67bl, 69bl, 74tl, 78bl, 80cr, 85cl, 112tr, 113cl, 114br, 118bl; /Glen Allison: 78cr; /David Austen: 73br; /John Beatty: 109cl; /Peter Cade: 85tr; /J F Causse: 81br; /Chris Cheadle: 79tl & 106tr; /Darrell Gulin: 95b; /Paul Kenward: 80tl; /Laurence Dutton: 117br; /David Hiser: 115bl; /Jerry Kobalenko: 88bl; /Hiroyuki Matsumoto: 69tr; /Alan Moller: 67br & 89tr; /Ian Murphy: 102tr; /Frank Oberle: 67tr; /Martin Puddy: 108tl; /James Randklev: 95cr; /Peter Rauter: 88br; /Jurgen Reisch: 78tr; /Lorne Resnick: 79bl; /Manoj Shah: 109tl; /Robin Smith: 69br; /Brian Stablyk: 79br; /Bill Staley: 100cl; /Vince Streano: 77tr; /Michael Townsend: 115tl; /Larry Ulrich: 67cl; /John Warden: 95tl; /Art Wolfe: 79tr; /Darrel Wong: 81tl. GSF Picture Library: 30tl. Robert Harding Picture Library: 9cl; /R Frerck(Odyssey;/Chicago): 51bl. Michael Holford: 20tl, 56t. Hulton-Getty: 8tr. Image Select: 26bl; /Caltech: 54b. JS Library: 58bl; /G Tonsich: 29cr. Landform Slides: 33cr. Mountain Camera/C Monteath: 55br; /J Cleare: 50t; /T. Kajiyama: 47br, 52t, 53cr. National Meteorological Library: 119tl. NHPA: /B&C Alexander: 115br. Oxford Scientific Films/V Pared: 9bl; /W Faioley: 55c. Planet Earth/Bourseiller&Durieux: 59t; /C Weston: 21tr, 32b; /I & V Krafft: 9tr & br, 27bl, 47cl; /J Corripio: 27cr; /J Waters page 11cl; /R Chesher: 14tr; /R Hessler: 15tl; /R Jureit: 38br; /WM Smithey: 36tl. Panos Pictures: 77b, 77cr, 93cr, 101cr, 108br, 109br & 109cr. Powerstock Zefa: 66br, 88tl, 93bl & 104bl. Rex Features: 26tl, 47bl, 48t, 63tr, 113b; /Pascal Fayolle: 112cr. Robin Kerrod: 70br, 81tr, 85cr, 96tl, 100bl, 101cl, 102cr, 113tl & 114tl. Science Photo Library: 9tl, 10tr, 15cl, 15bl, 15br, 18tl, 21tl, 21cl, 22c, 23cl, 42br, 76tr, 92tr, 93tl, 98tr, 104tr, 108bl, 119tr, 119br, 119bl; /Johnny Autrey: 105l; /Alex Bartel: 116br; /Tony Craddock: 95cl; /Gregory Dinijan: 72br; /Margaret Durrance: 89c; /Graham Ewens: 89bl; /Simon Fraser: 32t, 38t, 38bl, 39cr, 40tr, 71bl; /D Hardy: 33l, 42tl; /John Howard: 111b; /Phil Jude: 97bl; /Keith Kent: 99bl; /Peter Menzel: 47t, 119c; /Donna & Stephen O'Meara: 117tl; /A Pasieka page 34tl; /D Parker: 46t, 58t, 102bl, 105tr & 118br; /Pekka Parviainen; /Francoise Sauze: 90tr; /A C Twomey: 112bl. /D Weintraub: 30c; /G Garradd: 43c; /G Olson: 51br; /GECO(UK): 60t; /JL Charmet: 46b; /L Cook: 51cr; /NASA: 43b, 44t, 93br; /S Stammers: 44bl; /US Geological Survey: 44bl, 45t, 47cr. Spacecharts: 19cl, 27br, 30bl, 30br, 44br, 45c, 45b, 59bl, 80bl, 117tr & 118tl. Still Pictures; /A Maslennikov: 39t; /C Caldicott: 33br; /G&M Moss: 21cr. Stockmarket: 92b. Telegraph Colour Library: 24tl. Topham Picture Point: 31br, 55bl, 63cr. Tony Waltham: 10b, 11bl, 19t, 19br, 22b, 23bl, 27t, 31tl, 37tl, 39b, 43tl, 59br. Trip: 70bl & 120tl. Woodmansterne: 33tr.

Every effort has been made to trace the copyright holders of all images that appear in this book. Anness Publishing Ltd apologizes for any unintentional omissions and, if notified, would be happy to add an acknowledgement in future editions.